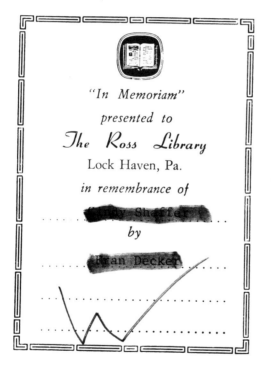

"In Memoriam"

presented to

The Ross Library

Lock Haven, Pa.

in remembrance of

.... ~~Ginny Shaffer~~ ....

by

.... ~~Fran Decker~~ ....

....

....

ARGENTINA

MAJOR WORLD NATIONS
ARGENTINA

Sol Liebowitz

CHELSEA HOUSE PUBLISHERS
Philadelphia

Chelsea House Publishers

Contributing Author: Jeff Beneke

Copyright © 1999 by Chelsea House Publishers,
a division of Main Line Book Co.
All rights reserved.
Printed and bound in the United States of America.

3   5   7   9   8   6   4   2

Library of Congress Cataloging-in-Publication Data

Liebowitz, Sol.
Argentina / Sol Liebowitz.
p.   cm. — (Major world nations)
Includes index.
Summary: Examines the geography, history, government, society,
economy, and transportation of Argentina.
ISBN 0–7910–4730–X
1. Argentina—Juvenile literature.   [1. Argentina.]
I. Title.   II. Series.
F2808.2.L54   1997
982—dc21   97–23551
CIP
AC

CONTENTS

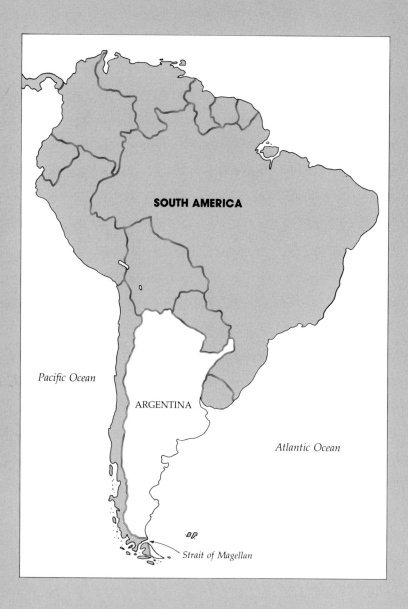

SOUTH AMERICA

Pacific Ocean

ARGENTINA

Atlantic Ocean

Strait of Magellan

BOLIVIA

Paraguay River

PARAGUAY

BRAZIL

Iguazú Falls

Tucumán

Santiago

Paraná River

Uruguay River

Córdoba

ACONCAGUA

Rosario

URUGUAY

Buenos Aires ★

Río de la Plata

Bahía Blanca

Viedma

San Carlos de Bariloche

Valdés Peninsula

PATAGONIA

Colonia Sarmiento

Falklands (Malvinas) Islands

Strait of Magellan

TIERRA DEL FUEGO

Beagle Channel

Ushuaia

FACTS AT A GLANCE

Land and People

Area	1,068,302 square miles (2,766,899 square kilometers)
Population	34,673,000
Population Density	32.5 people per square mile (12.5 per square kilometer)
Population Distribution	Urban, 87 percent; rural, 13 percent
Ethnic Groups	Europeans, 85 percent; Indians, mestizos, and others, 15 percent
Capital	Buenos Aires (population 2,965,400)
Neighboring Countries	Bolivia and Paraguay to the north, Brazil and Uruguay to the east, Chile to the south and west
Highest Point	Mount Aconcagua, 22,834 feet (6,962 meters) above sea level
Major Rivers	Río de la Plata, Paraná, Bermejo, Uruguay
Official Language	Spanish
National Holiday	May 25, the anniversary of the 1810 revolution

Religion	90 percent Roman Catholic; 10 percent other
Literacy Rate	96.2 percent
Infant Mortality Rate	28.3 per 1,000 live births
Average Life Expectancy	Men, 68.4 years; women, 75.1 years

Economy

Chief Imports	Machinery and equipment, chemicals, metals, fuels and lubricants, agricultural products
Chief Exports	Meat, wheat, corn, oilseed, manufactures; more than 50 percent of Argentina's export earnings are derived from agriculture.
Industries	Food processing, motor vehicles, consumer durables, textiles
Resources	Oil, lead, zinc, iron, copper, tin
Currency	The nuevo peso argentino, divided into 100 centavos

Government

Form of Government	Constitutional republic
Head of State	President, elected by popular vote
Legislative Body	Congress, divided into the Senate and Chamber of Deputies
Local Governments	23 provinces, 1 federal district of Buenos Aires

HISTORY AT A GLANCE

1516   Juan Díaz de Solís becomes the first explorer to enter the Río de la Plata region.

1536   Spanish establish settlement at what is now Buenos Aires.

1580   Buenos Aires is permanently resettled by Juan de Garay, after earlier unsuccessful attempts by others.

1609   The Jesuits set up their first mission, in northeast Argentina. For two centuries they attempt to convert the Indians to Christianity.

1600s   Buenos Aires develops into a leading port and an economic and cultural center.

1776   The Viceroyalty of la Plata is established by Spain. Buenos Aires is its seat; the viceroyalty includes regions of Argentina, Bolivia, Paraguay, and Uruguay.

Late 1700s   The Bourbons, the ruling house of Spain, initiate the Bourbon Reforms in an attempt to increase economic growth in Spain's colonies and extend Spain's control over the Río de la Plata region.

1800s Semiwild herds of cattle and horses roam the pampa, herded by gauchos, Argentine cowboys.

1806–7 British force attacks and occupies Buenos Aires, forcing the viceroy to flee; Argentine forces expel the British the following year and repel a second British force.

May 25, 1810 The revolution for independence from Spain begins in the Plaza de Mayo in Buenos Aires.

July 9, 1816 The United Provinces of La Plata are proclaimed, and independence from Spain is declared.

1819–20 Civil war breaks out between leaders from Buenos Aires, who want strong central government, and leaders from other provinces, who favor federal system of government; political turmoil continues into the 1830s.

1829–52 Juan Manuel de Rosas is the governor of Buenos Aires; his rule during these years becomes known as the "Rosas Tyranny."

1845 Domingo Sarmiento publishes *Facundo, or Life in the Argentine Republic in the Days of the Tyrants*.

1852 Rosas is overthrown by Justo José de Urquiza.

1853 Argentine constitution adopted; Argentine Republic proclaimed; Urquiza becomes first president.

1872–79 José Hernández's epic gaucho poem *Martín Fierro* gains popularity.

1877	The first ship with refrigeration chambers allows frozen beef to be shipped to England, sparking economic growth.
1912	The Radical Civic Union, a party favoring reform, first comes to power.
1914–18	Argentina remains neutral during World War I.
October 1945	Juan Perón takes control of Argentina with massive worker support. He is elected president in February 1946.
1955	The Peronist Period of 1943–55 comes to an end when the military takes control of the government. The military stays in power for the next 30 years.
1958	Argentina becomes the first Latin American nation to build a nuclear reactor.
1972	Juan Perón returns to Argentina after 17-year exile.
March 1973	Juan Perón is once again elected president. His third wife, Isabel Perón, is elected vice-president.
July 1, 1974	Juan Perón dies. Isabel Perón becomes president.
1976	A committee of military officers takes control of the government away from President Isabel Perón.
April 2, 1982	Argentine forces seize control of the Islas Malvinas (Falkland Islands), which are occupied by British citizens.

June 1982	Great Britain defeats Argentina and regains control of the Falkland Islands. Relations between the two nations are severed.
1983	Raúl Alfonsín is elected president.
September 1984	The famous *Nunca Más* (Never Again) report is released, detailing human rights violations committed by the previous military government.
1988	The inflation rate in Argentina nears 400 percent
1989	In May, Carlos Saúl Menem, leader of the reinvigorated Peronist party, is elected president. The next month, riots break out over skyrocketing food prices. Alfonsín, the retiring president, declares a state of siege and leaves office five months early. Menem adopts emergency policies to control inflation.
1990	Argentina and Great Britain restore diplomatic relations.
1994	Argentina signs the Treaty of Tlatelolco, promising to remain free of nuclear weapons. The same year, Argentina adopts a new constitution, which reduces the presidential term from six to four years and allows the president to seek a second consecutive term.
January 1995	With three of its neighbors, Argentina founds the Southern Cone Common Market (MERCOSUR).
May 1995	President Menem is elected to a second consecutive term.
March 1996	Menem is given emergency economic powers.

ARGENTINA

Buenos Aires, the capital of Argentina, is home to nearly 3 million people, making it the nation's largest city. Its location at the mouth of the Paraná River has made it a busy port, and its sophisticated residents are known as porteños.

1

Argentina and the World

Argentina is one of the most exciting and most troubled countries in the world. It is the second largest country in South America, and its people enjoy a high standard of living, excellent health-care programs, and one of the highest literacy rates in the world. (Over 96 out of every 100 people can read and write.) Yet its many military and political problems have led to a great deal of internal strife and economic difficulty. It is a beautiful, diverse land, rich in natural resources but also rich in controversy.

Argentina's landscape is as varied as its political and economic history. The Andes mountain range, which extends along the Pacific coastline of South America, rises on its western border. Patagonia, in the south, is a bare, windswept plateau; to the north is scrubland and tropical forests; and in the densely populated central area is the fertile, grassy plain called the pampa.

In the 18th and 19th centuries, the pampa was the home of the *gauchos*, South American cattlemen much like the North American cowboys. Like the cowboys, the gauchos became romantic figures in the popular imagination, symbols of self-reliance and rural dignity. Gauchos were mainly *mestizos* (people of mixed European and

Indian ancestry) who lived on horseback and traveled widely. But as immigration from Italy and Spain grew in the 19th century and the pampa region was divided into ranches and farms, this legendary figure was soon outnumbered by the influx of European settlers.

Most of the immigrants who did not choose to tame the pampa settled in Buenos Aires, Argentina's cultural and economic center and its capital. Today the Buenos Aires metropolitan area is home to nearly one-third of the nation's total population. In the 20th century large numbers of people have moved from the country to the city, and urban overcrowding, at its worst on the outskirts of Buenos Aires, has prompted the government to consider a new capital farther south in the city of Viedma, in Patagonia, to promote development of this largely desolate area.

The Indians were the first people to occupy the land that is today known as Argentina (named after the Latin word for silver, *argentum*). They were nomadic (wandering) fishermen, warriors, and farmers. European explorers, led by Juan Díaz de Solís and Sebastian Cabot, began coming to Argentina in the early 16th century. They soon established settlements, and one of the first was the Fort of Sancti Espiritus in the Río de la Plata basin in the central part of the country; it was destroyed by a surprise Indian attack in 1529.

Argentina's history since that time has been one of adapting European culture to the New World. More than perhaps any other Latin American country, Argentina reflects Old World values. This is especially true of Buenos Aires, with its imposing architecture, its almost exclusively European population, and its cultural and economic ties to Europe. The people of Argentina, called Argentines, speak Spanish and trace their colonial roots to Spain. Immigrants from Spain and Italy, as well as Jews from Eastern European countries and Germans, have peopled much of this land. Today, 85 percent of the population is of European descent.

Gauchos were the cowboys of South America. Just as with the cowboys of the old West in the United States, today there are more legends and stories about gauchos than there are working gauchos.

Another European country, Great Britain, has played an important role in the development of Argentina. Great Britain contributed greatly to the transportation system of Argentina by helping to build its railroad system. The British also introduced the English language and introduced the tremendously popular sports of tennis and polo. But it was also Great Britain that battled Argentina's military government in 1982 for control of the Falkland Islands (known in Argentina as the Islas Malvinas). The British victory and control over the islands led the countries to break off diplomatic relations until 1990. The military governments of the 1970s and 1980s provoked not only international troubles but also internal ones. Among the more prominent of these problems is that of los Desaparecidos (the Disappeared Ones, or missing persons). Los Desaparecidos are men and women in Argentina and other South American countries who have been taken into custody by their respective government because they disagree with its rule. Some of these dissidents have remained in custody for long periods of time or have been secretly tortured and executed, leaving relatives and friends uncertain of their fate. This violation of human rights received great international publicity in 1988 when a group of popular musicians, including Bruce Springsteen and Sting, toured the world to promote Amnesty International (an international human rights organization) and *The Universal Declaration of Human Rights*, a document that states that all people have basic human freedoms that should never be denied. Argentina allowed the final concert to be held at Río de la Plata Stadium in Buenos Aires, marking a new acknowledgment of the problem of human rights.

Mothers of los Desaparecidos (political prisoners secretly tortured or killed) gather in the Plaza de Mayo to demand information about their missing daughters and sons. Such protests inspired sympathy for the victims around the world and led to unprecedented trials and convictions of former junta members.

The military rule that was responsible for los Desaparecidos presents another of Argentina's main dilemmas, that of an ever-changing government. Although the current laws require democratic elections, Argentina's past has been littered with military takeovers and coups d'état (sudden, forcible overthrows of the government) that have prevented the country from maintaining a stable government that could effect change and accomplish more of Argentina's long-term goals.

Argentina's future rests on its ability to maintain a balance between urban and rural interests, to govern itself effectively, and to responsibly exploit its wealth of resources. Public education, health programs, and the standard of living in Argentina are all exceptional for a Latin American country. But the increased use of pesticides and chemical fertilizers and the problems accompanying oil and gas exploration threaten the beautiful natural life of Argentina, much as the possibility of a return to military rule threatens the freedom and self-expression of future generations. With thoughtful use of its resources and heritage, Argentina can become, like the sun on its flag, one of the brightest spots in the Americas.

At 22,834 feet (7,782 meters), Aconcagua is the highest peak in the Western Hemisphere. Part of the towering Andes mountain range, Aconcagua rises in Argentina near the Chilean border.

2

Geography

Argentina, the eighth largest country in the world, occupies most of the southern half of South America. It is the second largest country in South America (Brazil is the largest), with an area of 1,068,302 square miles (2,766,899 square kilometers), almost one-third the area of Europe.

Argentina's neighbors are Paraguay and Bolivia to the north, Brazil and Uruguay to the northeast, the Atlantic Ocean on the southeast, and Chile to the west and south. Its long western border with Chile stretches down almost half of South America, along the Andes mountain range.

Argentina is a country of great contrasts, varying from tropical forests in the north to the frigid peaks of Tierra del Fuego in the south. (Because Argentina is south of the equator, the north is warm; the south, cold.) In contrast to the flat plains of the pampa, the high mountains of the Andes reach far into the sky. From deserts to tropical rain forests, the federal republic of Argentina consists of 23 provinces and the Federal District (Buenos Aires). The province farthest south includes part of Antarctica, although Argentina's claim to this region is not recognized by the United States.

Early explorers were astounded by the size of the Andean condor, which can have a wingspan of 10 or more feet. Hunting in the 19th century and the destruction of its habitat in the 20th century have made it an endangered species, like its North American cousin, the California condor.

In such a large country, the climate, the vegetation, the animal life, and even the local cultures vary from region to region. The four main regions are the Andes, the north, the south (including Patagonia and Tierra del Fuego), and the pampa. Each has its own very distinctive geographical features, climate, and animal and plant life.

The Andes

The Andes mountain range, the longest on any continent, extends 5,500 miles (8,900 kilometers) from the southern tip of South America to its northern coast along the Caribbean and covers approximately one-third of Argentina. The Andes are not a single line of peaks but rather a complex system of mountains that often run parallel to each other, with plateaus and valleys lying in between. Because of the varying degrees of altitude, the Andean region has the widest temperature range in the country, with generally cold winters and hot summers.

In Argentina, the mountain system begins in the south on Staten Island, a part of the Tierra del Fuego Archipelago (an archipelago is group of islands). The range runs along the western border of Patagonia, where glaciers, lakes, and fjords (long, narrow inlets of the sea) are found. In this area, there is almost year-round snow on all the mountain peaks, and such popular resorts as San Carlos de Bariloche attract an international crowd of skiers. Farther north, the highest mountain in South America, Aconcagua (meaning "stone guard" in Indian dialect) rises. Its peak ascends to a height of 22,834 feet (6,850 meters) above sea level. In this region permanent snow covers only the peaks above 20,000 feet (6,100 meters), but few rise that high.

In the northwest corner of Argentina is the cold and desolate *altiplano* (high plateau), lying 11,000 to 13,000 feet (3,750 to 4,430 meters) above sea level. This region, which extends into Bolivia, is better known as the *puna* in Argentina. The climate is very dry and bleak. Little rain falls here, and the major sources of water are the rivers that begin in the snowfields in the mountains. These rivers carve out deep valleys called *quebradas*, which lead into the plains of the Chaco, a vast forested plateau in the northwest.

The puna is especially desolate and windswept, with few trees, some cacti, and much *tola* (a black shrub). Along the Andes to the south, beautiful conifer forests grow below the tree line and on the foothills.

Animals found in the puna region and farther south along the Andes include the vicuña, the alpaca, and the guanaco—all members of the camel family. The vicuña, the smallest, is a rare species that is hunted for its fine wool. It lives in groups of 5 to 15 animals, composed of 1 male and a number of females. Foxes, chinchillas, eagles, pumas, and the impressive Andean condor, which is now a threatened species, also live in the wild in this area.

The Andean condor and its North American relative the California condor are the two largest flying birds in the world. The Andean condor's wingspan can reach 10 feet (3.4 meters) or more, and the bird is approximately 4 feet (1.4 meters) in length. It feeds primarily on carrion (the flesh of dead animals) and breeds every other year high in the mountains, leaving two small white eggs in a nest, where they incubate for seven weeks. The newborn condors cannot fly for the first year of their life. Although they do not have a superb takeoff, condors are very graceful fliers, using the strong thermal winds off the mountains to soar high above the land in search of food.

The North

The north contains the following three areas: the Chaco, or "hunting grounds," Argentine Mesopotamia, and the tropical rain forests in the northeast. Mighty rivers run throughout the north, which covers approximately one-third of Argentina. The Paraná and the Uruguay rivers flow into the Río de la Plata. The Chaco is crossed by the Bermejo, Dulce, Salado del Norte, and Pilcomayo rivers.

The Chaco is a region of savannas (grass-covered plains) and forest. The *quebracho* tree grows thick in this area and is used to make tannin (which is used for tanning hides). Heavy rainfalls cause widespread flooding during the summer, but the winters are much drier. The Chaco receives about 30 inches (750 mm) of rain each year.

Mesopotamia is a humid lowland area that stretches between the Uruguay and Paraná rivers. In the southern part there are rolling grassy hills, or *cuchillas*, and swampy valleys. The Paraná River floods yearly and restricts settlements to higher ground. To the north, the wooded swamps of Mesopotamia merge with the tropical and subtropical forests of the northeast. The fertile soil of

Graceful guanacos are related to llamas and vicuñas but grow larger. Llamas and vicuñas have continued to thrive in Argentina because their silky wool is in demand for making clothing.

Mesopotamia provides ideal growing conditions for thick groves of talas, palm, mimosa, and carob trees.

In the Chaco and in Mesopotamia the climate is hot and humid where weather from the north prevails. In the winter there are frequent cold spells caused by the invasion of Antarctic air from the south. (In regions south of the equator the seasons are the opposite of those in the Northern Hemisphere—it is summer in December and winter in June.) The summer is very hot and wet, and the winters are generally dry. The average temperature in the Chaco is 74° F (23° C), but it can reach a high of 116° F (47° C) in the summer. Mesopotamia's average temperature is about 70° F, and in the winter the humidity reaches 90 percent.

The fauna (animal life) of this part of Argentina is truly fascinating. Armadillos, capybaras (the largest rodents in the world, sometimes weighing more than 110 pounds, or 50 kilograms), otters, and tapirs can be found in the north, and in the province of Jujuy alone there are jaguars, pumas, roe deer, coatimundis, monkeys, and tapirs. The

Iguazú Falls, near Argentina's border with Brazil, is the central attraction in a huge national park that preserves more than 135,000 acres (54,675 hectares) of tropical jungle. Rain forests elsewhere are threatened with destruction.

armadillo and the coatimundi are two of the most interesting creatures that roam the country. The armadillo is a nocturnal mammal (it sleeps during the day) that lives within a shell of armor made up of bony plates. In fact, the name comes from the Spanish and means "small armored one." The coatimundi is a long-nosed member of the raccoon family that keeps its tail swaying high in the air as it travels through forests and plains. Along the Paraguay and Paraná rivers are found flamingos, herons, and parrots. The Chaco shares much flora (plant life) and fauna with the puna. The abundant wildlife in this area includes the vizcacha, the puma, the ferret, the chinchilla, the armadillo, the otter, the guanaco, and the vicuña.

On the border with Brazil are the fantastic Iguazú Falls, twice as wide as Niagara Falls in North America, discovered in 1541 by Alvar Nuñez Cabeza de Vaca. They are surrounded by tropical jungle and are part of Iguazú National Park, a vast reserve of 135,905 acres (55,000 hectares), with one of the highest jungles in the world. The reserve shelters more than 400 species of birds, pumas, and many types of fish, such as the *peces tigre*, a typical river fish. The falls themselves look like endless foam crashing through the trees and falling amid rainbows on sunny days.

The northeastern forests are also home to monkeys, colorful butterflies, marsh deer, coatimundis, and jaguars. The huge tapir, from 6 to 8 feet (1.8 to 2.5 meters) in length and 3 feet (1 meter) high , is a shy resident of these forests, traveling on well-worn paths that make it easy prey for man and jaguar. This relative of the horse and rhinoceros families is rare in Argentina today because of destruction of its habitat and overhunting.

The South

With its low-lying shrubs and windswept plateaus, Patagonia covers most of the Argentine south, which as a whole accounts for more than one-fourth of Argentina. Its southern limit is the Beagle Channel, named after the British ship HMS *Beagle*, in which naturalist

Charles Darwin, the principal developer of the theory of evolution, sailed and explored the area in 1832–33. The eastern part of the channel forms the border between Argentina and Chile.

The large island of Tierra del Fuego (Land of Fire) was named after the campfires of the Ona and Yagane Indian tribes, which were seen by the first Europeans who passed by the island. Today it is divided between Chile and Argentina. At the foot of Argentina's territory is Ushuaia, the southernmost city in the world and the gateway to Argentina's claim to Antarctica. North of this city the snow-clad peaks of Tierra del Fuego are visible, along with its sparkling rivers, waterfalls, and dense forests. To the south are the green waters of the Beagle Channel.

A treaty signed in 1985 seems to have ended almost a century of conflict between Chile and Argentina over control of some of the small islands in the Beagle Channel. Both countries agreed to allow the Vatican, a neutral party, to examine their dispute and recommend a solution. Argentina has agreed to uphold the decision of the Vatican, which appeared to favor the Chilean claims. Chile gained control over the Picton, Lennox, and Nueva islands. Both countries now have rights to the surrounding ocean.

An important part of the southern section of Argentina is the Antarctic Peninsula, a region of 372,426 square miles (599,606 square kilometers), which is used by the Argentine government mostly for weather and scientific observations. Beautiful red-crested Adélie penguins roam the coasts here, and some of the few remaining blue whales swim the ocean.

The Islas Malvinas, or Falkland Islands, are windswept, remote, and treeless, covered only with low shrubs. Despite its defeat by Great Britain, Argentina still claims these isolated islands. The islands are sparsely populated. British sovereignty has been in effect since the end of the Falklands War.

In Patagonia (the name comes from *Patagones*, a term used by early Spanish explorers for the original inhabitants), the winters are cool (averaging approximately 35°F) and the summers mild (70°F) for its latitude. Moisture-laden winds from the west drop most of their precipitation over the Andes, creating what meteorologists call a "rain shadow," which keeps most of Patagonia very dry, with an average yearly rainfall of approximately 5 inches (125 millimeters) at Colonia Sarmiento. The harsh climate encourages little vegetation other than short grasslands and monte (drought-resistant scrub bushes). The short grasslands on the plateaus of Patagonia are ideal for raising sheep, and numerous shepherds lead their flocks across this bleak region.

In Neuquén Province open bushland is most common, with grasses and widely spaced thickets reaching a height of three to seven feet. Closer to the Andes, where rain falls more frequently, enormous

Flocks of Adélie penguins clamber over the rocky shores of the Antarctic Peninsula, part of Argentina's claims in Antarctica.

trees, resembling the sequoias of the northwestern United States, grow in ancient forests.

The Valdés Peninsula is a large nature reserve on the Atlantic Coast, home to a populous colony of elephant seals. Male elephant seals reach a length of about 21 feet (6.5 meters) and a weight of about 7,770 pounds (3,530 kilograms); the females are somewhat smaller. The seals feed on fish and squid and are most aggressive during the mating season, when the males fight to attain territories and harems of 13 to 30 females. The females produce a single offspring yearly. Like elephant seals in California, the Argentine elephant seal has been hunted for oil, but it is now under government protection. Also on the peninsula can be found rheas (large ostrichlike birds), Patagonian hares, fur seals, gray foxes, and guanacos.

The Pampa

The pampa is located in the heart of Argentina. The region, which makes up about one-fifth of Argentina, acquired its name from the Quechuan Indian term meaning level land. The pampa is a flat, seemingly endless plain that covers an area of approximately 403,000 square miles (650,000 square kilometers). Amid these flatlands are three *sierras* (low ranges of hills): the Sierras del Tandil (1,640 feet, or 500 meters), the Sierras de Córdoba (4,920 feet, or 1,500 meters), and the Sierra de la Ventana (3,936 feet, or 1,200 meters). But other than these ranges, the pampa is a monotonously flat sea of grass, broken at long intervals by the trees, windmills, and barbed wire introduced by European settlers.

The humid pampa stretches south of Buenos Aires along the coastline and has fertile land, with enough yearly rainfall to grow most crops with only limited irrigation. When the Europeans first arrived, this part of the pampa was covered with tall, coarse grass. European pasture grass has since been planted throughout this region to improve the diet of grazing cattle and horses.

The Valdés Peninsula is home to herds of huge elephant seals.

On the dry pampa, where humidity averages 76 percent, sand dunes and mounds of dirt dot the flatlands. These mounds of dirt are created by the vizcachas that abound in this region. The vizcacha is a small burrowing rodent that spends most of its day in the ground and comes out at night to forage through the grasses. Vizcachas are often prey of the pumas that wander the remote pampa.

The pampa was rich in wildlife before Europeans introduced fertilizers, pesticides, and insecticides. The area was home to many

The flat pampa stretches for miles in the heart of Argentina. Much of it looks as it did in the 19th century, when only the gauchos on horseback and their herds of cattle and sheep, along with scattered clumps of trees, stood out against the broad horizon.

species of birds, including the rhea, the thrush, the stork, the beautiful black-necked swan, and the weird chaja, or screamer, so called because it screams when large animals approach. The chaja can swim like a duck and fly for hours at great heights. Partridges, doves, and owls are also found on these flatlands.

This entire area is affected by the *pampero*, a violent southwest wind that races across the plains and clears the way for much-needed rainstorms. The pampa has warm summers and mild winters, with only occasional snow or frosts. The average temperature is 60° F (16° C). The rainfall varies from about 38 inches (975 millimeters) in the humid pampa near Buenos Aires to 22 inches (550 millimeters) in the dry pampa at Bahía Blanca.

The natural environment of the pampa has been noticeably altered. Mile after mile, travelers see herd upon herd of cattle, horses, and occasional sheep or hogs on the rolling plains. These European species, developed for livestock raising, have displaced much of the native fauna in these regions, and fences have restricted the freedom to roam of remaining indigenous animals.

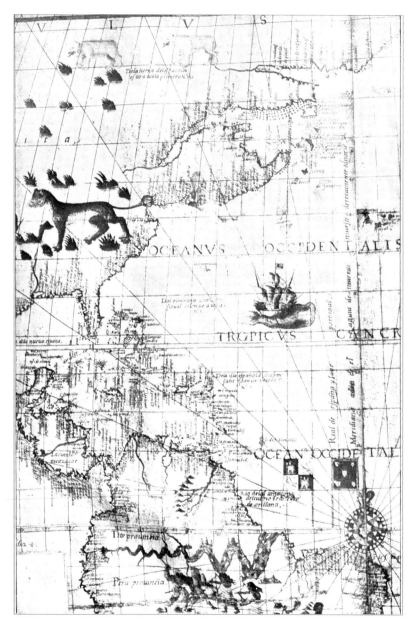

In 1544, Sebastian Cabot completed this map of his many explorations of the New World, which included a voyage in 1526 to the area of present-day Argentina.

3

History Through the Nineteenth Century

Argentina was originally inhabited by Indians, who are believed to be descendants of Asians who crossed the Bering Strait in prehistoric times and gradually spread throughout the Americas. It is estimated that approximately 300,000 Indians were living in the area now known as Argentina when the early European explorers arrived.

The Spanish found no vast Indian civilizations in Argentina like those of the Aztecs in Mexico and the Incas of Peru. The organization, culture, and structure of the Indian groups and the relationships between them varied throughout the area and were in a constant state of change. Most of the inhabitants lived in nomadic tribes, with few permanent settlements and no written literature.

The northwest mountains were inhabited by the Calchequíns, a tribe of warriors who battled the Inca Empire, which was centered in Cuzco, high in the Andes of Peru, and stopped it from spreading south into the Argentine region. The Diaguita, one of the more advanced of the Indian tribes, also resided in the northwest. They were experienced with both ceramics and metals and built irrigation dams. Another tribe, the Chiriquano, were Guaraní-speaking Indians who inhabited the Gran Chaco, a terrain of forested plains that spreads throughout much of South America; they survived mostly as nomadic fishermen and hunters. The Moliche Indians lived in Patagonia. On Tierra del Fuego, the Ona, Yahgan, and the Alikuf Indians lived in tribes that were left in possession of the island until 1880, when Argentines and Chileans introduced sheep farming and began looking for gold.

One of the earliest explorers to make his way to Argentina was Juan Díaz de Solís, a Portuguese navigator employed by the Spanish crown. In 1516 he became the first explorer to enter the Río de la Plata estuary, where an arm of the sea meets the mouth of the river. He sailed up the Uruguay River and was attacked by the Charrúa Indians in what is now Uruguay. He and all but one of the rest of the landing party were killed and eaten as the remaining members of the crew watched in horror from the ship. Ferdinand Magellan, while on his journey around the world in 1520, entered the Río de la Plata, turned back and continued south down the coast, and then sailed through the strait that now bears his name, at the southern tip of the continent.

One of the most important explorers to set foot on what was to become Argentina was Sebastian Cabot, an Italian who was born and raised in England but sailed under the Spanish flag. He had been commissioned to develop trade to the Orient, but he was distracted by rumors of tremendous deposits of silver in the Río de la Plata region. (It was he who gave the river its name, which means the River of Silver in Spanish.) Beginning in 1526, Cabot spent three fruitless years in search of fortune. After traveling the full length of the Río de la Plata, he and his men set up camp at Sancti Espiritus along the river Paraná before being forced out by the Indians. Upon his return to Spain, he was banished to Africa for not completing his mission in Argentina, but two years later he was pardoned.

Permanent colonization was attempted by Pedro de Mendoza, who founded Ciudad de Nuestra Señora Santa María de los Buenos

Aires (City of Our Lady Saint Mary of the Fair Winds) in 1536. Mendoza's expedition, composed of more than 1,600 men, sailed across the Atlantic on 16 ships. But the large size of the party, more than three times the number that Cortés brought to Mexico, became a major problem because there was little for them to eat at this site.

Mendoza, ill with syphilis (a venereal disease) and disheartened by the disappearance of a party of men who had left to explore the interior, decided to return to Spain with most of the survivors. Those who remained fought off increasingly hostile Indians until they moved upriver to Asunción in Paraguay. Later attempts to rebuild Buenos Aires were unsuccessful, and the site was soon abandoned. Although Mendoza's settlement of Buenos Aires failed, Argentines still recognize him as one of the founding fathers of the country. The Province of Mendoza in the Andes is named after him.

When the Spanish abandoned Buenos Aires, they left some of their horses there, which greatly affected the Indian way of life. Horses that escaped from this area as well as from other settlements drastically changed the life of the Indians on the pampa. The Indians

Ferdinand Magellan sailed through the strait that bears his name at the southern tip of Argentina on his trip around the world in 1520. Until the opening of the Panama Canal in the 20th century, the strait was part of the round-the-world route for vessels such as this steamship.

captured these horses and soon became excellent riders; they used this newfound skill to rustle cattle and steal other horses. The horse thus became the first major economic and cultural influence that the Spanish brought to the native population.

The Spanish continued to move into the area, forcing the Indians to move out. Spaniards from Chile, Peru, and Paraguay were among the first European settlers in Argentina. During the 16th century, cattle that had been set loose across the country adapted very well to the pampa habitat. Excursions into the grasslands by *vaqueros*, men who hunted wild cattle, were common, and the vaqueros provided settlements with meat, clothing, and even shelter, for many huts were covered with cowhide roofs.

As cities developed, so did their organizational structure, which was overseen by the viceroy of Peru, Francisco de Toledo, an agent of the Spanish crown. Food and wages were regulated, and both the church and *los cabildos* (town councils, or local governments) shared governing responsibilities.

After the early failures to colonize Buenos Aires, the area was permanently resettled by Juan de Garay in 1580. But for almost two centuries after Solís's discovery, the southern half of South America remained of little importance to the Spanish crown. The viceroy of Peru governed all of what later became Argentina as well as the rest of the Spanish settlements in South America. But because of the wealth he acquired from plundering the vast and gold-laden Inca Empire in the north, the viceroy paid little attention to the southern half, which had no appreciable mineral resources and an Indian population that could not be easily enslaved.

Following closely behind the Spanish settlers were the Jesuit missionaries, who came to Argentina in an effort to convert the Indians to Christianity. In the north, the Spaniards fought to compel the Indians to become Christians and placed the docile natives under forced labor. The province now known as Misiones in northeast Argentina was so named because of the large number of Jesuit

In 1526, Sebastian Cabot became the first European to sail up what he named the Río de la Plata (River of Silver), but he failed to find any great stores of precious metals. Nevertheless, his Spanish backers continued to send adventurers and colonists to the area.

missions that were established there by the 18th century. The Jesuits set up their first mission in 1609 and converted almost all of the Guaraní tribes in the northeast region but were not successful with the nomadic tribes to the south. These Indian tribes were being pushed farther west as the area around Buenos Aires was being settled, so life on the frontier continued to be dangerous for the settlers, with Indian raids a constant threat.

Wars between the Indians and the Spanish settlers were numerous in the 1600s. The two periods of fiercest fighting were the 1630s between the Spaniards and the Diaguita and from 1657 to 1659 between the Spaniards and a group of Indians led by the Spanish

The first settlement of Buenos Aires failed, but a later effort in 1580 was successful. A contemporary drew this sketch of Buenos Aires in its early days.

rebel Pedro Bohórquez, who fought for control of the Calchaquí Valley of the northwest. The Indians once again were defeated, and Bohórquez was captured and eventually executed in Peru in 1667.

The years from 1680 to 1810 saw the impressive development of Argentina's most important city, Buenos Aires. Because the Spanish crown sought complete control over all exports of gold and silver from its colonies, the only port legally open to trade was in Peru. The early growth of Buenos Aires was due in part to the vast amount of illegal trading of slaves for silver that the inhabitants pursued. This clandestine trading helped the humble village of the late 16th century become one of the greatest commercial centers in Latin America.

It was not until 1776 that the Viceroyalty of la Plata was established (including present-day Argentina, southern Bolivia, Paraguay, and Uruguay) and the region was able to rule itself, although still under the jurisdiction of the Spanish crown.

A new dynasty, the Bourbons, gained control of the Spanish monarchy in 1776 and authorized reforms of the colonial government, in order to make the colonies self-sufficient, while also creating stronger markets for Spanish goods and providing more raw materials for the parent country. The new policies called for increased local economic growth through expanded trade and also set up *intendencias*, small territorial governments that controlled taxation, land claims, and economic development.

There were many cultural changes in the city of Buenos Aires during this period. *Estancias* (large estates), which were almost always owned by Europeans, were established. These European owners employed mestizo gauchos, who often survived on meat and *yerba mate* (a tealike herbal drink) alone, to care for their herds of semiwild cattle. Toward the end of the 18th century, tenant farmers began to plant wheat in the valleys along the Paraná-Plata

Horses and cattle were unknown on the pampa until a few escaped from Spanish encampments. Finding abundant grasslands for grazing and no natural enemies, they soon multiplied and their semiwild descendants provided a living for the gauchos.

44

shore, bringing agriculture to this region of Argentina for the first time. The gaucho and the *estanciero* (the owner of an estancia), both of whom lived off the free-roaming cattle herds, were opposed to this planting.

Throughout colonial times, Buenos Aires and the rest of Argentina had to fight against Spanish policies that limited the great independent economic progress the region was attempting to establish; the Bourbons were determined to see that it was the Spanish crown that got rich, not the Argentines under its rule. But even before the viceroyalty had been implemented, the Buenos Aires cabildo often acted with daring independence, trying to break free from its European domination.

Independence

In 1803, Great Britain was at war with France, then ruled by Napoléon, and with Spain, France's ally. Their aggression extended to Spain's colonies as well. In 1806, British invaders under Sir Home Popham, who acted without the official backing of the British government, took over the city of Buenos Aires. The *porteños* (the people of the port of Buenos Aires) themselves began the popular and successful movement to rid the city of the British, and they even

repelled a second invasion in 1807. These victories helped to boost the self-confidence of the Argentines in their efforts to become independent of Spain. When Napoléon invaded Spain in 1808 and named his brother Joseph king, Spain's colonies in the Americas, including Argentina, were further encouraged to fight against Spanish rule, which was quickly weakening.

Thoughts of independence began to circulate among the people, and on May 20, 1810, the inhabitants of Buenos Aires gathered in the Plaza de Mayo to demand that a *cabildo abierto* (open town meeting) be held. On May 25, the cabildo set up a junta (group of leaders) to rule the colony. (The official date of the revolution is May 25, which has since become a national holiday.) It was this revolution, which originated in the Plaza de Mayo in Buenos Aires, that began the quest for independence throughout South America. José de San Martín, known as "the George Washington of Argentina," was the preeminent leader of the Argentine independence movement. He also organized revolutions in Chile (1817) and Peru (in 1821, aided by Simón Bolívar, who helped Venezuela gain its independence).

The independence movement created new problems for Argentina. Following six years of heavy fighting, with Spain externally and between Artigas (rebels who demanded local self-government)

Buenos Aires had become one of the busiest ports in South America by the 1800s. During the previous century, it was a center of smuggling and illegal trading, but its size and prosperity made it the natural choice for the capital of the Viceroyalty of La Plata, established in 1776.

and Unitarists (conservatives who supported a national union) internally, the independence of the provinces of the Viceroyalty of La Plata was declared at the Congress of Tucumán on July 9, 1816, and the United Provinces of La Plata was proclaimed. The unfortunate consequence of independence, though, was continuous civil war. Much of the conflict occurred between Buenos Aires and the provinces. Whereas the porteños were Unitarists who preferred centralized power, those of the rural areas were Artigas, who wanted to give the provinces local governmental control.

San Martín was the great *creole* (person of European descent born in the colonies) hero of the South American independence movement. He did the most to bring about the declaration in Tucumán and was called "the Saint of the Sword" for his unselfish, virtuous qualities. After the success of his fighting for independence throughout South America, San Martín left Buenos Aires, disturbed

José de San Martín led the fight for independence from Spain in South America, not only in Argentina but also in Chile (with Bernardo O'Higgins) and Peru (with Simón Bolívar).

This monument in the Plaza de Mayo is inscribed with the official date of the beginning of the revolution, which has since been declared a national holiday, much like the Fourth of July in the United States.

by the rivalries in his native country, and lived in France until his death in 1850. His remains were returned to Buenos Aires, where they were buried in the Buenos Aires cathedral on the Plaza de Mayo.

A democratic constitution (calling for presidential elections, a congress, and separation of powers) was adopted in 1826, although some Argentines had wanted to establish a constitutional monarchy and appoint a king. The constitution was based in part on that of the United States. The constitution, however, did not curb tensions in the country.

Domingo Faustino Sarmiento's tenure as president of Argentina from 1868 to 1874 was a period of great economic progress. He reorganized the public education system, supervised the building of railroads, and strongly encouraged immigration from Europe and foreign trade.

The Argentine Nation

General Juan Manuel de Rosas was governor of Buenos Aires from 1829 to 1832. From 1835 to 1852, he was Argentina's first dictator. Using the slogan Long live the Argentine Federation, he attempted to unite the nation under his rule. He did not follow the constitution and ruled with absolute authority. Rosas also interfered with the affairs of neighboring countries: He prevented the union of Peru with Brazil and tried to impose a pro-Argentine government in Uruguay. Despite his bloody tactics (he was known as "the Caligula of the Rio de la Plata," after the notoriously brutal Roman emperor) and his tendency to exile his opponents, he never achieved the Argentine unity that he had so violently attempted to bring about.

The Indians of the pampa survived mostly as hunters, and the Spanish never succeeded in altering the Indians' way of life in order to absorb them into their culture. Thus there were constant battles for the pampa. The Europeans and creoles eventually succeeded in wiping out most of the tribes. The remaining Indians were driven to the far west or to small reservations.

After the Indian wars, many officers were given large tracts of land of more than 98,880 acres (40,000 hectares) each. It was through this granting of large estancias that the pampa passed into private hands.

After the success of the Indian wars, Argentina began to be transformed into a country of whites instead of mestizos. Such leaders as Juan Bautista Alberdi (author of the 1853 constitution), Bartolomé Mitre (president 1862–68), and Domingo Faustino Sarmiento (president 1868–74) encouraged massive European immigration. Sarmiento, deeply impressed by the North Americans' successful extermination of the Indians and subsequent white domination, wrote many books on his plans for Argentina. *Facundo, or Life in the Argentine Republic in the Days of the Tyrants*, perhaps his most famous and important work, called for urban and European dominance over rural, peasant barbarism.

Together Sarmiento and Mitre helped to undermine Rosas's brutal precedent and established Buenos Aires as the cultural and political center of Argentina. To Sarmiento, Buenos Aires was the outpost of civilization in the midst of a wild land. In his opinion, the gauchos and the Indians led lives that belonged to a bloody past, and both Mitre and Sarmiento wanted all traces of their culture removed and replaced with one of porteño calm and sophistication. Ironically, more bloodshed was needed to achieve these goals.

Despite the uprisings, anarchy, and war, Argentina developed a strong economy during the 19th century. The pampa continued to open up as railroads were established with the aid of foreign technology and capital. Settlements as far west as Mendoza in the Andes grew into cities filled with new immigrants from France and Italy, who changed the economy from one based on cattle raising to a region renowned for its wines. Refrigerated steamships, which permitted Argentine beef to be shipped across the ocean, and advances in animal breeding, which improved agricultural production, helped Argentina face the new century as a modern nation. European immigration, mostly from Spain and Italy, changed the country's population from largely mestizo to largely white by the 20th century.

The most influential Argentine politician in the 20th century was President Juan Perón. He and his charismatic wife Evita rode through the streets of Buenos Aires in triumph after his reelection in 1952.

4

Peronism and the
Twentieth Century

Argentina's most important economic advances were made in the late 19th century and the early part of the 20th century. But during this time, the nation's political development failed to match its economic and social progress.

Some political strides were made with the formation of the Radical Civic Union in the 1890s. Supported largely by Spanish and Italian immigrants and the urban middle class, this party was able to elect its candidate to the presidency in 1916, after President Roque Sáenz Peña made elections more open by forcing Congress to pass laws allowing universal male suffrage (the right to vote for all adult males) and the secret ballot. Before this time, conservative landowners and military forces had controlled the government. In 1918 young college students started La Reforma, the university reform movement, which reorganized higher education and laid the groundwork for social and political change. This movement established Argentine youth as a healthy and rebellious part of society, although all too often the political activism of the country's young people has put them at great personal risk under the more oppressive regimes.

In 1916, the Radical Civic Union, to which the majority of Argentines belonged, elected Hipólito Irigoyen president. His time in office was marked by expanded social welfare and education programs.

Argentina's problems continued after the Radical Civic Union party leader Hipólito Irigoyen was elected president in 1916. His rule was characterized by internal battles with Congress and the Conservatives and was troubled by worker strikes, civilian vigilante groups, and accusations of improper government spending. Even so, Irigoyen was extremely popular because the majority of the population were Radicals; he ruled until 1922, when his six-year term ended, and ran again in 1928, when he once again became president.

The Conservative party and high-ranking officers in the army took control from Irigoyen and the Radicals in 1930 in a coup d'état, led by General José F. Uriburu, that set another political precedent for Argentina in the 20th century. This party managed to stay in power for 13 years by violently repressing all dissent and by arranging for many elections, especially rural ones, to be fraudulent.

It was not until the end of the 1930s and the outbreak of World War II that Argentina began to experience the serious economic difficulties of the Great Depression. This economic slowdown had devastated other nations after the crash of the New York stock market in 1929. With much of Europe at war in 1939, many of Argentina's export markets were closed off, and unemployment began to grow. With agricultural exports down, the rural population moved to the urban centers, and Argentina's industrial labor force doubled (as the agricultural work force dwindled), reaching about 1 million workers in the period between 1935 and 1946. However, there were not enough jobs for these displaced agricultural workers. As a result, the urban slums mushroomed, especially on the outskirts of Buenos Aires.

During the 1930s, Argentine leadership seemed to be in disarray. Control of the government bounced back and forth between the Conservative party and the Radicals; leaders such as General Augustín P. Justo were accused of falsifying ballots and of bribery; and serious battles were waged for control of Congress and the governorship of the capital city of Buenos Aires. The 1938 election was won by Radical Civic Union member Roberto Ortiz, and by 1940 the Radicals regained control of the Chamber of Deputies for the first time in 10 years.

Conservatives saw increasing tension in the new labor force as a threat to political stability and viewed the growing membership of the Communist party with alarm. The military thought President Ramón Castillo (an open admirer of Spanish dictator Francisco Franco and Italian dictator Benito Mussolini) and the Radical-Socialist Congress were unable to control the unrest. On June 4, 1943, the military staged a coup and installed civilian rule. The military also restricted the labor movement, arrested political opponents from all parties, and censored the press.

Labor reform was long overdue in Argentina, and it was time for a new voice to arise amid the repression. This voice came from one of the most dynamic figures in all Argentine politics, Juan Domingo Perón, riding high on the crest of a new populism, a popular movement to restore government to the people, including the working class.

The Rise and Fall of Perón

Juan Perón was at once a reformist, a Fascist (a believer in dictatorship), a despot (a ruler with absolute power), and to some Argentines, a saint. He was born in the small village of Lobos, 50 miles (80 kilometers) outside of Buenos Aires, on October 8, 1895. He studied medicine in school but later switched to a life in the military, where he rose from cadet to captain to a professor of military history. In 1940 he was a military attaché in Mussolini's Italy, where he admired the parades, the speeches, and especially the marching Blackshirts (as the supporters of Mussolini were called because of the color of their clothing). He took these favorable impressions of fascism back with him when he returned to Argentina later that year.

Perón was appointed head of the National Labor Department in October of 1943 and helped to unite the various labor unions, then torn by constant disputes. His supporters grew in number as he pressed for retirement pensions and minimum wages. At this time he began courting Eva Duarte, later to be known as Evita, who helped him in his upward climb. Duarte was a glamorous, popular actress who voiced strong opinions supporting women's rights and charity and was extremely attractive to most Argentines; her popularity increased Perón's own popularity dramatically.

By late 1945, Argentines from the Communists to the Conservatives, as well as the triumphant Allies of World War II, were opposed to the shaky military regime that had ruled since Castillo was ousted. The most recent in a long line of leaders had been General Edelmiro Farrell, who first had appointed Perón minister of war in 1944, then later dismissed and imprisoned him because of scandal and resentment of his power by other military leaders. But Perón was not to be silenced for long.

In October 1945, with the backing of the workers and the young military officers of the government, Perón came to power in front of a sea of Argentines who had filled the Plaza de Mayo with their waving banners and shirtless bodies, calling for his release. Los

Juan Perón inspired violent emotion among Argentines. His devoted supporters turned out in massive crowds for celebrations honoring him during his first period in power in the 1940s. The church, conservative landowners, and military officers formed his powerful and bitter opposition.

Evita Perón had been a popular actress before her marriage to Perón; after his election, she organized a wide-ranging social welfare program and often spoke at public functions on behalf of her husband and his policies.

Descamisados (the Shirtless Ones), as Perón's followers came to be called, were ecstatic. Farrell embraced Perón, recognizing both his power and that of los Descamisados. Farrell and General Eduardo Avalos, the leader of the military opposition against Perón, may have formally been in charge of the country, but Argentina was now all Perón's. Four days after Perón became Argentina's unofficial leader, Eva Duarte, who had so greatly helped his rise to power by appealing to the masses with her popularity, became Perón's second wife. (He was a widower.) Avalos resigned (which later led to the military reconciling with Perón, as he gave them pay raises and appointed them to important managerial posts in order to gain their favor), and

Farrell quickly called for elections to be held in February 1946; Perón won the election with 54 percent of the vote, making him president of Argentina.

The period just after World War II saw Perón at the height of his power as he united the military with a popular alliance and began to protect the interests of Argentine industry. The February 1946 elections had officially given Perón the presidency, a large majority in the Congress, and control over most of the provinces. He earned the nickname *el Líder*, derived from the English word *leader*. During his first stay in power (1946–55) he established voting rights for women and brought the labor unions increased political say and credibility. The opening of markets in postwar Europe initially caused an upward surge in the Argentine economy. Perón's pension and welfare systems attracted Argentines from all factions to his movement.

In 1947, Perón launched the first of his five-year plans. During this period, the railroads (formerly owned by Britain), the telephone and gas works, the urban transportation systems, and the centralized bank all were nationalized (put under government control). Through programs set in motion by his five-year plans, Perón sought to achieve economic progress under a system midway between capitalism (private ownership) and communism (a classless society that features common ownership).

While in office, Perón also began to harass his opposition. For example, he influenced Congress to impeach anti-Peronist Supreme Court judges in May 1946 and in 1947 began closing down anti-government newspapers such as *La Vanguardia*. Claiming that intellectuals were obstacles to the new order, he dismissed more than 1,000 members of Argentina's teaching staff at the universities. He also used propaganda to maintain the support of the workers and restricted freedom of the press. In 1949 his officials seized *La Prensa*, the leading independent newspaper, which was not returned to its owners until after he was deposed in 1955.

Eva Perón continued to be an important leader in her own right and assisted Perón throughout his career. She supported the popular democracy that he had advocated during his rise to power. But after her death from cancer on July 26, 1952, at the age of 33, Perón's regime grew more conservative and repressive. However, without his charismatic wife, Perón lost much of his support among the people.

At first he wooed the favor of the church by establishing mandatory Roman Catholic education in the public schools, which all students had to attend. But his courtship was temporary, and the church and the students became greatly opposed to Perón's regime. He forced teachers to take political tests and revised the textbooks in order to promote Peronism. Farmers were also reluctant to support him, because he favored industry and thus did little to help agricultural workers. During this time, migration from the country to the city continued to increase.

The United States, hoping to keep markets in Europe for its own products, prohibited European nations from using U.S. aid money to buy agricultural products from Argentina. This restriction may have been in part a reaction to Perón's anti-imperialism actions, which were directed primarily against the United States and Great Britain. Perón proclaimed Argentina's "third position," which supported limits on English and American influences but did not embrace the Soviet Union in their place. An example of this attitude was the creation of the Agencia Latina, an organization that suppressed North American and British cultural influences while trying to promote specifically Argentine and South American culture.

In the 1950s, Perón began an anti-Catholic crusade that further divided his supporters. By mid-1954 he had caused a major rift between him and the church by insisting that the government dominate charity organizations and the education system the way the church had done previously. Perón did this with the intentional desire of undermining the church's power. Another reason for the church's disapproval of Perón was because of his supposed relationships with young teenage girls following the death of his wife.

Perón recognized that he was losing the support of some segments of Argentine society. On July 15, 1955, he called for national unity and suggested the end of Peronism. With his power quickly slipping through his fingers and internal fighting worsening, he took one last stand and addressed the public on August 31, calling out *"Cinco por uno"* ("Five for one") and announcing that he would kill five anti-Peronists for every Peronist that was killed. Civil war was at hand.

Less than one month later General Eduardo Lonardi, supported by military forces in Córdoba as well as by the landowners and the Roman Catholic church, led a military revolt that forced Perón to resign under the threat of a combined naval and army rebellion. To

Argentine women achieved the right to vote in 1947, aided by Evita's vigorous support for women's rights.

60

prevent further civil unrest, Lonardi called his coup a revolution of liberty that had no winners or losers.

Perón took refuge on a Paraguayan boat and left behind a Peronist-controlled labor movement and political party as well as millions of followers. Throughout his exile he exerted his influence over Peronists and non-Peronists alike, never really leaving the hearts of many Argentines.

The importance of the military has been emphasized over and over again in Argentina's history. Throughout the period of Perón's

Throughout Perón's 17-year exile (1955–72), his supporters and opponents vied passionately for power in Argentina. In 1966, the government forbade pictures of Perón to be shown in public; as soon as the ban was lifted in 1971 Peronists plastered walls with posters proclaiming "Nothing without Perón!"

exile, much violence occurred as the military tried to destroy not only Peronism but all opposition. In the early 1970s torture was a standard technique for police interrogation.

Although the Peronists were not in control for almost 20 years, they toppled many governments. The military so feared Perón's influence that even displaying his picture was against the law for several years. However, over time some Argentines recalled Perón's first presidency with increasing fondness. Perón himself spent his exile in various Latin American countries with governments similar to his own, such as General Alfredo Stroessner's Paraguay and Fulgencio Batista's Cuba. But after 17 years of exile, he returned to Argentina for a short time and almost immediately began to exert his power. In March 1973 free elections were held, and the Peronist alliance known as the Justicialist Liberation Front took control of the government by winning the presidency. Perón was welcomed back with wild enthusiasm. But not all Argentines were happy with his return, and there was much violence and protest. Despite these protests, on September 23, 1973, at the age of 78, he was reelected president, receiving 62 percent of the popular vote. His third wife, Isabel, was elected vice-president.

By 1974, after having pledged to support both the military and the Radicals alike, Perón began to betray the latter, and arrests and assassinations took place. As always, he was operating more from a military viewpoint than from a democratic one. Political unrest was inevitable.

On July 1, 1974, Perón died, and his wife succeeded him as president, making Isabel Perón the first woman head of state in the Western Hemisphere. She lacked Evita's popular charm and attraction, however, and her presidency immediately alienated most Argentines. High inflation (rising prices) and terrorist activities (including robberies, kidnappings, bombings, and assassinations) severely threatened the Peronist government.

After Juan Perón's death in July 1974, his vice-president and third wife, Isabel, suc-ceeded to the presidency and stayed in office for almost two years, until yet another coup expelled her from power. These soldiers stand before the Casa Rosada a few days after the March 1976 military takeover.

In 1976, amid charges of corruption (she was accused of taking money from a public charity for personal use), the armed forces ousted President Perón and began a military junta (a group of ruling military officers) that lasted for almost a decade. This regime was perhaps the harshest in Argentine history. The military refused to compromise with any opposition parties and, in an effort to control the economy, restricted the power of labor unions and banned all strikes.

At this time, antimilitary and human rights groups were guer-rillas in a conflict known as the Guerra Sucia (Dirty War), in which they battled the armed forces for three years before being virtually wiped out. This period was followed by a long economic decline and the refusal of the military to return the government to civilian rule. Inflation during this decade of military rule was the worst in the world. What a single peso would have bought in 1974 cost 15,000 pesos in 1983.

The ruthless murder of thousands of Argentines known as los Desaparecidos soon began to come to the attention of the rest of the world. These opponents of the military government were often secretly arrested and then tortured and murdered. But repression and recession could not last forever, and the military regime came to a spectacular demise.

The Falkland Islands War and Democracy

In March 1981, General Roberto Viola was appointed president by the junta but was forced to resign in December following a coup by General Leopoldo Galtieri, who insisted on a strong central government and used the slogan Firmness and Action to guide his rule. During these years, economic conditions were growing more severe, exerting greater pressure on the military. As a result, there was almost constant war with all citizens who were opposed to Galtieri's dictatorial rule. The Communists and leftists had already been destroyed by the late 1970s, and Galtieri, now facing weaker internal opposition (much of his opposition had been silenced through mass murders and disappearances), turned to conflicts with foreign forces to maintain his regime's militant momentum.

Argentina provoked border conflicts with Chile and eventually waged a full-scale war against Great Britain. Claiming that the Malvinas (Falkland) Islands were transferred to Argentina at the time of independence from the Spanish crown in 1816, Argentine forces seized control over the islands on April 2, 1982. The islands had been seized by Great Britain in 1833 and had remained British territory since then, although Argentina laid claim to them throughout its history as a nation. The Argentine invasion of the Falklands in 1982 shocked the world, and the Argentine people united beneath the call of anti-imperialism. The cry "Las Islas

A woman gazes at a pile of human bones, wondering whether her son's are among them. The military government of the 1970s and early 1980s secretly tortured and killed thousands of its political opponents.

Malvinas son Argentinas" ("The Malvinas Islands are Argentine") was heard throughout the country. It was the first open conflict between troops and foreign forces in more than 100 years; the previous confrontation had been a bloody war that pitted Paraguay against the combined forces of Argentina, Brazil, and some Uruguayans as a result of political strife in Uruguay.

Great Britain retaliated strongly, to the surprise of most Argentines, who expected it to back down. On May 21 a large British force landed on East Falkland Island. Within 2 weeks Britain had brought a large naval force to the area, and in a total of 72 days, the war was over, at a cost of 2,000 casualties and U.S. $2 billion. On June 14, Argentina agreed to a cease-fire, and Argentine forces withdrew

President Leopoldo Galtieri ordered the invasion of the British-held Falkland Islands in 1982 to distract Argentines' attention from the economic disorder and human rights violations under his military rule.

from the islands less than a week later. The war ended almost 200 years of trade between Argentina and Great Britain.

From the beginning it was evident that the war was used for political gain on both sides. The British prime minister, Margaret Thatcher, used it to maintain a zeal for her conservative government and to recall fond memories of the great British empire that had finally fallen apart in the 20th century. The Argentine leader General Galtieri needed an aggressive action to direct attention away from his harsh rule and the shambles of the economy, and the battle with Great Britain gave him a perfect opportunity to do so. He also had the support of all Latin American nations except Chile, whose leader Augusto Pinochet supported the British.

Great Britain's success helped to topple the military regime, and Galtieri resigned, leaving the reputation of the Argentine army seriously wounded. After the loss, the Argentines shifted their focus to another very grave problem, that of los Desaparecidos.

In September 1982 the police were ordered by the junta to ban all discussion of los Desaparecidos on radio and television. As elections were planned for 1983, a newspaper interview with General Ramón J. Campos, a former chief of police, revealed the horrible truth, for he proudly boasted of his fight against subversion and claimed that all los Desaparecidos were dead.

Elections in 1983 gave Raúl Alfonsín, a lawyer from the city of Chascomus, and his Radical Civic Union an absolute majority in the electoral college and Congress. His claims that Peronists had collaborated with the military junta helped to win the election. He revealed a secret pact between the head of the Peronist unions and the commander of the military that stated that the military would help the Peronists get elected if investigations into los Desaparecidos were halted. The Peronists were willing to accept the murders, Alfonsín claimed, whereas his party would prosecute. He later upheld his promise by forming CONADEP, the National Commission on Disappeared Persons. Jorge Luis Borges, a world-famous

Argentine writer who rarely spoke of politics, claimed that the date of the elections, October 30, was "a historic date that gives us law, a sense of duty and hope."

In September 1984 the new democratic government released a report on human rights violations of the military government in the 1970s. The report was called *Nunca Más* (Never Again) and led to an unheard-of process in Latin America: holding the military accountable for its human rights violations. Generals began to stand trial for the cruelties they had ordered. But some complained that the sentences these generals received were too light and that too few of them were actually brought to justice. During Alfonsín's tenure, eight high-ranking military officers, five of whom had been mem-

Raúl Alfonsín, president from 1983 to 1989, oversaw the preparation of Nunca Más, *a report on the abuses of the previous military government, but was unable to bring Argentina's economy under control.*

Carlos Menem, elected president in 1989, faced a daunting array of problems and a dizzying inflation rate when he took office in June.

bers of military juntas and two of whom were former presidents—Jorge Videla and Roberto Viola—were tried, convicted, and sentenced.

Despite Alfonsín's popular success, he still could not control the Peronist unions or the military, and his government was running into trouble by the end of 1987. Perhaps most damaging to his popularity was the government's failure to control the disintegrating economy. Spiraling inflation, widespread unemployment, and shrinking wages fueled the union-backed Peronist party's rise, and its candidate, Carlos Saúl Menem, won the presidential elections held on May 14, 1989. Peronist party members won a majority of seats in the Senate and half the seats in the lower house of the legislature, ensuring that Menem would face little legislative opposition to his policy of "productive revolution," a plan to reinvigorate the economy by granting widespread wage increases and making it easy to borrow money.

Although Alfonsín's was the longest-lasting Argentine civilian government in 40 years and the 1989 election marked the first time in 60 years that power had passed legally from one popularly elected president to one of another party, the transition was not peaceful. Two weeks after the election, the capital erupted in violent riots over skyrocketing food prices. Alfonsín declared a constitutional stage of siege, then resigned June 30 to allow Menem to take power five months before the scheduled date.

Argentina faced chaos, and the new administration went right to work. In an effort to establish some economic stability, Menem imposed an austerity program. He sought to balance the budget, cut government spending, and encourage foreign investments in Argentina. Menem convinced commercial banks to reschedule payments of the country's enormous debts, and he sold many state-owned enterprises to private investors.

In an attempt to reduce the size and power of the armed forces, Menem cut the military budget sharply. At the same time, he pardoned six commanders in chief of the armed forces who had been convicted of serious human rights abuses during the Dirty War.

In 1994 Argentina adopted a new constitution, which permitted Menem to be re-elected as president in May 1995. Facing yet another economic crisis, Menem was granted emergency powers in March 1996, allowing him to impose new taxes without congressional approval. Because of such frequent troubles, Argentina's economic and political future remains uncertain.

The cabildo (town council) building in downtown Buenos Aires, where the group that declared independence from Spain in 1810 met, currently houses a museum of national history.

5

Government and Society

The government of the Argentine Republic (República de Argentina) seems to be in a constant state of change. During its recent history it has operated under militarism, Peronism, and democracy, and virtually every new decade has ushered in new leaders with different messages. Following the Falkland Islands War in 1982, the military leadership that had ruled for the previous eight years called for a new election and a return to the form of government proposed by the Constitution of 1853, which was based in large part on the U.S. Constitution. Eventually, under the civilian governments that followed, a revised constitution was adopted in 1994.

Under the current constitution, the government is headed by a president who serves a four-year term. The 1994 revision allowed the president to seek a second consecutive term and also removed the constraint that the president be a Roman Catholic. The president is elected by universal suffrage; voters must be at least 18 years old.

The president serves as the chief executive and commander in chief of the armed forces. The president is also responsible for appointing all cabinet ministers and military and judicial officers. He or she may also pardon or commute the sentences of citizens found guilty of federal crimes.

Like the United States, Argentina has a Congress that handles the legislative aspects of the government. The Argentine Congress consists of 2 houses made up of representatives from the 23 provinces, and the Federal District, which encompasses Buenos Aires. The upper house, the Senate, has 72 members, with 32 members from each of the provinces and Buenos Aires. The Senate is presided over by the vice-president, who is elected in the same manner as the president. Senators serve nine-year terms. The lower house, the Chamber of Deputies, is made up of 257 members, and each of the provinces sends a number of representatives to the chamber based in its population. Deputies serve four-year terms.

Each of the 23 provinces and the Federal District retains all powers that are not explicitly granted to the federal government. Under the military regimes, the national government often appointed provincial governors and interfered in other ways with local government. Since the return to constitutional rule, the provinces have been governed by their own institutions, and they elect their own governors, legislators, and other officials.

The judicial branch of government is headed by the Supreme Court, which is made up of nine judges appointed by the president. All Supreme Court and federal judges are appointed for life. The court system also consists of five appellate courts as well as local provincial courts.

Much like the constitution of the United States, the Argentine constitution sets up a system of checks and balances on both the national and local levels, resulting in a separation of power among the executive, legislative, and judicial branches of government.

The Argentine Constitution is similar to the U.S. Constitution in many other ways. Like the U.S. Bill of Rights, it guarantees the people freedom of speech and religion and the rights of public assembly and private property. Constitutional amendments in 1957 and 1972 gave the people the right to bargain collectively and to strike,

(continued on p. 81)

(Overleaf) An Argentine Indian spins thread with a coya *high in the Andes near Salta, in the northern part of the country.*

The celebration of Argentina's Independence Day is marked with military parades. The military has always played a major role in Argentine history and politics.

The Band of Grenadiers of San Martín parades and performs while on horseback.

Grapes are one of Argentina's many agricultural exports. This vineyard is near Mendoza in the region that produces some of Argentina's best wines.

The fertile pampa of Argentina stretch for miles in the heart of the country, providing pasture for Argentina's vast herds of cattle.

Argentine children can take advantage of an excellent school system. Nearly one-third of the nation's population is under the age of 14 and so entitled to free education under the Argentine constitution.

A white obelisk marks the crossing of Avenida 9 de Julio and Avenida Corrientes in the Plaza de la República at the center of downtown Buenos Aires.

*Opera and theater performances at the world-renowned Teatro Colón in
Buenos Aires draw enthusiastic audiences from all over Argentina.*

A ship docks at a pier in Ushuaia, the world's southernmost city. Located in the Argentine part of the Tierra del Fuego, the city's 42,000 residents live 650 miles (1,040 kilometers) from the South Pole.

(continued from p. 72)

the right to receive adequate housing and support for the family unit, and the right to obtain a minimum salary, paid vacations, and a pension.

One major difference, however, between the U.S. and Argentine constitutions is that the Argentine constitution does not declare a strict separation between church and state. The Roman Catholic church enjoys state protection, although freedom of religious belief is granted to all other denominations. The president even has the power to appoint Catholic bishops. The Catholic church has at times been deeply involved in politics. For example, it claimed responsibility for both the success of Peronism starting in 1943 and the end of that period of Peronism in 1954.

The responsibility for maintaining law and order is shared by several law enforcement agencies. The Federal Police, Border Police, and Coast Guard all report to the interior minister. Governors have the responsibility for overseeing the police forces in their provinces. According to the U.S. State Department, some provincial policemen continue to commit human rights abuses.

The armed forces consist of the army, navy, and air force. In 1995 compulsory military service was abolished, and the number of men in the military was reduced. For the past century, the military has frequently been a major force in Argentine politics. Each time it seized control of the government, however, it was forced to surrender its role as a result of its own problems running the government. The last time it did so was following the Falkland Islands War, when the military leaders returned power to civilian rule and held elections in 1983 that were won by Alfonsín of the Radical Civic Union.

The military government agreed to the elections for three main reasons. One was the loss of the war to great Britain. A second was its failed economic policy. The third reason was that many of the men in charge of the military government were involved in a systematic abuse of human rights involving los Desaparecidos that drove the people against military rule.

The Radical Civic Union is one of the primary political parties in Argentina. It was founded in 1892 by merchants, factory workers, and tenant farmers. The second major party is the Justicialist party, formerly known as the Peronist party, which is supported by organized labor. This party, which was in power from 1946 to 1955 and from 1973 to 1974, unexpectedly rose to prominence in the late 1980s. In fact, the winner of the 1989 and 1995 elections was Carlos Saúl Menem, a Peronist who toured the country in a luxury bus and posed in magazines wearing bathing suits. Although his sponta-

The dome of the congressional building rises beyond the lawns of the Plaza del Congreso. Argentina's two-chamber legislature has had a varying degree of influence on the country, depending on the type of government in power: military junta or elected representatives.

Argentine federal court chambers were packed with spectators and newspeople in April 1985 at the sentencing of several of the eight military officers who were tried, convicted, and jailed that year for human rights abuses and illegally repressing dissent.

neous style made him a new kind of politician, many of his ideas stemmed from those of Perón, except that Menem claimed to represent a more democratic type of Peronism. Other smaller parties include the Union of the Democratic Center, a conservative party; the Grand Front, a center-left coalition, and the right-wing Movement for Dignity and Independence.

Since civilian governments regained control in 1983, they have expanded Argentina's involvement in world politics. Argentina became a member of the Contadora Support Group, joining with Brazil, Peru, and Uruguay in an attempt to further the peace process in Central America. Argentina also signed the Treaty of Tlatelolco, which calls for the peaceful development of nuclear energy. Argentina has worked to improve its relationship with the United States as well as with countries it borders, such as Brazil and Chile. This was made evident when Chile and Argentina signed a treaty peacefully settling their dispute over the islands in the Beagle Channel. Argentina is also a member of the Organization of American States, the United Nations (since 1952), the Latin American Integration Association, the Inter-American Treaty of Reciprocal Assistance (the Rio Treaty), the Southern Cone Common Market, and the World Trade Organization.

Health and Education

Argentina has one of the best health records in South America. The life expectancy for men is 68.4 years, and for women it is 75.1 years. (Life expectancy refers to the number of years a baby can expect to live.) The infant mortality rate (the number of children who die before their first birthday) is 28.3 per 1,000 live births, and the maternal mortality rate (the number of women who die as a result of childbirth) is 100 per 100,000 live births. The population growth rate is 1.1 percent, which is quite low. The total population was estimated to be 34,672,997 in 1996. The population density is 32.5 people per square mile, or 12.5 people per square kilometer. The major causes of death are heart disease, cancer, accidents, and childbirth-related problems. The daily per capita caloric intake is 131 percent of the Food and Agricultural Organization minimum.

Argentina has more doctors per capita than any other country in Latin America. There is 1 physician for every 376 citizens. In comparison, Brazil has 1 doctor for every 715 people, and the United States has 1 for every 391 people. Argentina also has 1 hospital bed for every 227 citizens.

Many of the public hospitals provide free medical services, and trade unions often have medical and dental plans for their members. Further health assistance is provided by the government through the Ministry of Social Welfare. At the end of 1983, Alfonsín began the Programá de Alimentación Nacional (PAN), a national food program that provided subsidies in an attempt to prevent any people in Argentina from going hungry.

Argentina places an extraordinary priority on the education of its people. The government spends approximately 14 percent of its annual budget on education and education-related programs. Over 96 percent of Argentines over the age of 10 can read and write, giving Argentina one of the highest literacy rates in the world. The 1853 constitution made education free and compulsory, so all children between the ages of 6 and 14 are required to attend school. The school year runs from March to December, and Argentine children get their two-week winter holiday in July. Besides their native Spanish, many Argentine children also learn French, English, and Italian.

Military forces have often intervened in Argentine politics during both bloody and nonviolent coups. No president in the 20th century has been able to accomplish his objectives or even remain long in power without the backing of the military.

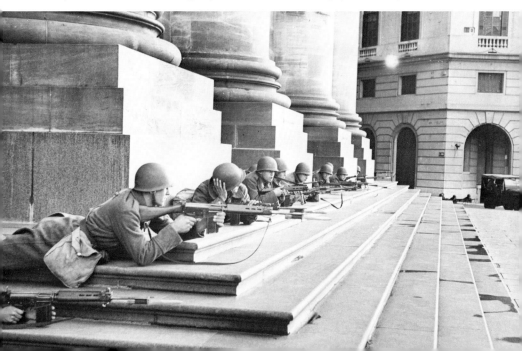

Argentine children have enjoyed excellent free public schooling since 1853, when the constitution created the educational system. Less than 4 percent of Argentines older than 10 cannot read or write.

The importance Argentina places on education is also apparent in the number of schools, teachers, and students in the country. There are more than 25,000 primary schools (for students ages 6 through 12); 7,000 secondary schools (for students ages 13 through 17); 31 state universities; and 1,700 other institutes of higher learning. The primary schools have 287,000 teachers and 5.1 million students, so there are 17.8 students per teacher. In comparison, in the United States there are 18.3 students for every teacher. The secondary schools have 233,600 teachers and 2.3 million students, so there are 9.8 students per teacher, compared to 14.8 high school students per teacher in the United States. The small number of students per teacher allows more individual instruction and promotes more student involvement in the process of learning.

Córdoba was the first university founded in Argentina, in 1613. The University of Buenos Aires is the leading institution of higher learning. Others include the Catholic University of Argentina and universities in Bahía Blanca, La Plata, Mendoza, Tucumán, and Rosario.

Shoppers throng the streets of a busy pedestrian mall in Buenos Aires.

6

Economy, Transportation, and Communications

Although Argentina is one of the most developed countries in South America, high inflation and government mismanagement have prevented it from becoming a wealthier world power. The average yearly income is barely enough to survive on. This was the result in part of the spread of unemployment and wage controls imposed in a vain attempt to control the inflation that plagued the country. The unemployment rate in Buenos Aires was 20 percent in 1995; for the country as a whole, it was 18.5 percent. Argentina is neither poor nor underdeveloped, but the average Argentine income is low because the country's economy suffers large-scale problems, one of which is the enormous amount of money owed to foreign banks.

Argentina's economy remains very dependent on agriculture, even though only 13 percent of the people live in rural areas. Agriculture accounts for more than half of the country's earnings from exports. The agricultural industry employs 12 percent of the work force and accounts for 6 percent of Argentina's gross domestic product, or GDP (the total value of goods and services produced within a nation). Argentina's major crops include wheat, corn, and soybeans, and it is among the leading grain and wheat producers in the world. Its wealth of fertile lands, especially the pampa, and its climate have allowed Argentina to become self-sufficient in food production. Argentina has become a major tea producer and has developed successful apple, citrus fruit, and wine industries.

Argentina has long been one of the largest producers and exporters of beef in the world. Most of its cattle are raised on the pampa. In recent years, however, beef exports have fallen sharply, and much of the agricultural production has been shifted from livestock to crops. The number of cattle in Argentina declined from about 57 million in the 1970s to 50 million in the 1990s. Argentina also breeds significant numbers of sheep, goats, pigs, and chickens. Sheep raising is particularly important in the southern region of Patagonia.

In the 1980s, the cereal and beef industries were hurt by competition from other countries. Farmers faced heavy taxes on food exports and high expenses for imported fertilizer. In addition, the European Community, now known as the European Union (an economic association of western European nations), put limitations on the amount of food that its members could import from Argentina, further affecting the farmers. Argentina also lost an important customer for several years following the Falkland Islands war when diplomatic relations with Great Britain were disrupted. By the mid-1990s, the Menem administration was promising that deregulation of the economy and reduced barriers to free trade would improve agricultural income.

The service industries produce 63 percent of Argentina's GDP and employ 57 percent of the work force, mostly in local, state, and federal government jobs (including military posts) and in the banking system. Manufacturing industries, which employ 31 percent of the work force, produce another 31 percent of the GDP. Following agriculture, textiles, metals, lumber, fishing, and mining are among the most important Argentine industries.

Argentina is rich in natural resources that make it energy self-sufficient. The country produced 210 million barrels of oil in 1993, and it produces enough natural gas to supply its own needs with some to export as well. Until the early 1990s, the development, refinement, and transportation of oil and natural gas were financed by the government. Today, a huge network of oil and gas pipelines helps supply the urban industrial centers with energy. Argentina also boasts large uranium reserves and in 1958 became the first country in South America to build a nuclear reactor. Nuclear power

Argentina's vast herds of cattle have made refrigerated and frozen beef Argentina's prime export for more than 100 years.

The fertile plains of Argentina yield such abundant crops that it is able not only to feed its own people but also to export large quantities of grains and meats.

supplies about 13 percent of the country's electrical needs. In the 1970s and 1980s, large hydroelectric projects were begun on the Paraná and Uruguay rivers. The first of 20 generators at Yacyreta were activated in 1994, and Argentina now relies on hydroelectricity for more than one-third of its power.

Argentina imports about the same amount of goods as it exports. Agricultural products account for over half of the total export value. Among the leading export commodities are meat, cereals, fruits and vegetables, oilseed, and manufactured goods. Some of the major imports are machinery, chemicals, metals, and fuels and lubricants. Twenty-one percent of Argentine imports come from the United States. Other major sources of imports are Brazil, Germany, Bolivia, Italy, and Japan. The United States, Brazil, Italy, Japan, and the Netherlands are Argentina's primary export markets.

Argentina's industrial development has been limited for many reasons. One major problem is that a large percentage of its industry is located in and around Buenos Aires. Another problem stems from past government involvement in industry. From the 1940s through the early 1990s, the government owned large portions of many major industries and had a monopoly on railroads and utilities. These government-controlled industries accounted for about half of Argentina's GDP, but most were inefficiently managed. In addition, the use of outdated machinery and severe labor unrest (including many strikes) lowered overall industrial profitability.

Government ownership of Argentine industries also made imported merchandise more expensive. The government imposed high tariffs designed to raise the price of imports so that they would not compete with goods produced by government-owned industry. For example, if the government owned a steel factory, it would place a tariff on imported steel to ensure that its price was not significantly less than the price of government-owned steel. This slowed industrial growth by raising the price of materials needed to start up

Riot police guard the burned-out remains of a train wrecked during a violent railroad workers' strike. Argentina's powerful labor unions have gained many benefits for employees; they have also been responsible for many crippling strikes.

A young salesman displays a sign announcing that all credit card purchases have been suspended as a result of government action to control the economy.

and run a business. Today, most government-owned industries have been turned over to private companies, but by the mid-1990s there was little indication that industries would grow as a result.

The investment market has also affected industry. Argentina has a huge foreign debt: It owes more than U.S. $90 billion to international banks. This has kept foreigners from investing money in the Argentine economy, although President Menem has taken steps to reassure foreign investors. Meanwhile, many Argentines have also become fearful of their own economy and instead have invested in foreign markets. Their mistrust of the Argentine economy stems from the Peronish period of the 1940s, when Argentina's debt first started to balloon. During this time, the country began printing money in order to finance its growing industry; the result was a large debt and an exorbitant inflation rate. This high rate of inflation has led people to spend what they have instead of saving for the future; it has also induced many Argentines to exchange foreign money in for the illegal black market instead of through the government. (The black market frequently offers better exchange rates.)

The Alfonsín government attempted many new measures in order to turn Argentina's debt around. One of the first things it did was to replace the peso with the austral as the national unit of currency. But the austral's value declined quickly, so in 1992 the Menem government introduced the nuevo peso argentino. This "new Argentine peso" has maintained an exchange rate of 1 peso equal to U.S. $1.00. Menem also implemented many drastic measures aimed at improving Argentina's economy, and for a time it looked like he was succeeding. The inflation rate fell dramatically, and both foreigners and Argentines began investing in domestic industries. The economy experienced another crisis in 1995, however, as unemployment soared and investment levels fell off.

Transportation and Communications

Buenos Aires is the transportation hub of Argentina and one of the world's most important seaports. The railroad system, which was owned and operated by the government until 1992, links the capital city to the rest of the country with 23,560 miles (37,910 kilometers) of tracks. Argentina has 133,980 miles (215,578 kilometers) of roads, but only 28 percent of them are paved. There are 4.3 million cars on these roads, as well as 1.5 million commercial vehicles and buses. Another major form of travel is by water, and Argentina has a complex waterway system that runs through the Uruguay, Paraná, and Plata rivers. Air travel is also available with Aerolineas Argentinas, the national airline that was privatized in 1990, as well as several smaller airlines. The primary airport is in Buenos Aires.

Argentina is a very well informed nation, with a daily newspaper circulation of 143 per 1,000 citizens. A complex telegraph system also links the country together. Buenos Aires is the country's information center. The capital has 14 major daily newspapers, including *La Prensa*, an important paper that covers international news extensively, and *La Nación*. The most important English-language newspaper in South America is the *Buenos Aires Herald*. The nation is also the home of numerous well-respected Spanish-language literary journals and reviews, and it has a large book publishing industry.

Argentina has at least 75 privately owned radio stations and another 37 that are controlled by the state. By the mid-1990s there were about 23 million radios in the country, or about 1 radio for

Argentina's extensive railway system includes this impressive feat of engineering—a 738-foot-long bridge that rises 210 feet above the ground. The railroad line links Argentina's oil-rich northern region with the Chilean port of Antofagasta, to the west of the Andes on the Pacific Ocean.

La Prensa *is one of the most renowned newspapers in South America. Independent since its founding in 1869, it was seized by Juan Perón in 1951. This photograph depicts a vendor selling the first issue of the paper published freely in 1956, when Perón was overthrown and the daily resumed independent publication.*

every 1.5 people. Argentina also has over 230 television stations (both private and state controlled), but there are many fewer television sets than radios—about 1 television for every 4.8 people. By comparison, in the United States there are 2 radios for every resident and 1 television for every 1.2 residents. Similarly, by some estimates, Argentina has 1 phone for every 8.2 people, whereas in the United States the number of phones is quickly approaching the number of people. These figures indicate that, as rich in resources as Argentina is, many families still live without such modern conveniences as televisions and telephones.

The distinctive dress costumes of the gauchos, including a long silver-handled dagger and a belt made of rows of silver coins, are now worn only at historical reenactments and festivals.

7

Life in Argentina

The rich cultural life of Argentina springs from numerous sources. Its culture is diverse, but two important groups have influenced the entire country: the gauchos, both by their legend and reality, and the porteños, the people of Buenos Aires.

The gauchos, or Argentine cowboys, have been highly romanticized in Argentina and are an integral part of its folklore. Most were mestizos who roamed the open plains as horsemen and cowhands throughout the 18th and 19th centuries.

Their literature and their habits are well known to Argentines, who begin to learn about their country's past in grade school. The great epic poem *El Gaucho Martín Fierro*, by José Hernández, is studied throughout Argentina and recalls the actions, the daily life, and the passions of the gauchos on the pampa. Hernández was one of the first Argentine writers to defend the gaucho and to write of the hardships and eventual doom of the gaucho way of life. In schools, parts of this poem are often memorized by students for recital.

The *pulperías* played an important role in the world of the gaucho. They were general stores where the gauchos would go to buy whiskey and the goods that they needed to survive. Scattered throughout Argentina, they stocked items such as wine, spirits, salt, bread, candles, firewood, and other important merchandise such as yerba mate, a drink that is as much a part of Argentine culture as are the people who drink it.

Yerba mate is a tealike drink first prepared by the Indians from leaves they collected from wild shrubs and trees in the north of Argentina. Its sharp taste made it popular among the gauchos, for it added variety to their diet—they lived almost exclusively off the roaming herds of cattle they tended. It is prepared by placing the dried leaves in a hollow gourd and pouring hot water over them, then allowing them to steep briefly. The gourd is passed around a group of drinkers, who sip it through a *bombilla* (a metal straw) inserted in the gourd. This tradition persists to the present day, and Argentines gather for mate drinking in large apartments in Buenos Aires as well as in small cinder-block houses on the pampa.

The story of the gaucho has been greatly romanticized during the decades following his disappearance (much like legends of the cowboys in the Old West in North American culture), and some tales are more myth than fact. However, a gaucho did possess one indisputable quality: fine horsemanship. The gaucho used this ability to hunt free-roaming herds of cattle and horses that had escaped from ranches and adapted very well to the pampa, where they had no natural enemies. He majestically rode his horse through the pampa bearing his lasso, his bola (a triangular weighted weapon, often made of leather and stones, used by horsemen to catch animals), and his spare saddle. This horseman was master of all that he saw from horizon to horizon, encompassing an endless sea of grass and sky. From sunup to sundown he could always be found in his saddle.

At the end of the 18th century, the pampa was divided into estancias, and for approximately 50 or 60 years the gaucho continued to be employed as a skilled animal handler. But as estancia owners began to fence in their property at the end of the 19th century, the gaucho way of life was doomed, and it became the basis of legend. Purebred domesticated cattle from Europe replaced the half-wild herds, and owners used their land more efficiently. The gaucho, once so free, was forced to become a farmhand, living within a particular estancia not unlike the animals, which were now limited to grazing the land between the fences of the estancia.

The importance of rural life has been limited in 20th-century Argentina, for along with the United States, Argentina has become one of the most urbanized countries in the West: More than half of all Argentines live in cities and towns of more than 20,000 people.

Working gauchos have been a rare sight since the beginning of the 20th century, but they remain enduring romantic figures in popular culture.

In the 1921 silent movie
The Four Horsemen of
the Apocalypse,
Rudolph Valentino
portrayed a young Argen-
tine and tangoed with his
partner. The movie made
him a star and spread the
popular craze for the dis-
tinctive Argentine dance.

The porteños, 12.5 million strong, are the most influential city dwellers in Argentina, and it is from them that much of the nation's government and intellectual life come. The porteños are regarded by the rest of the country as sophisticated and modern. Some spend their afternoons in luxurious 19th-century cafés or in small bars engaging in philosophical conversations about the state of the world or about the last horse race at Palermo, the world-renowned racetrack in Buenos Aires. Historically, they have had more direct contact with Europe and North America, so they often set the trends and filter new ideas through to the provinces.

In Buenos Aires, as in the rest of Argentina, the language predominantly spoken is Spanish. The official language, it is taught in all Argentine schools and is the only one used by the government. However, one almost exclusively porteño dialect, Lunfardo, strongly influences the daily language in the capital. This dialect, composed of words borrowed from Portuguese and Italian, originated around 1900. It is associated with the underworld and the music of the tangos.

The heart of Buenos Aires since the colonial days continues to be the Plaza de Mayo, enclosed by the cabildo, where the movement for independence from Spain was first begun; the Casa Rosada (Pink House), which is the president's official home; and the cathedral, where the South American liberator San Martín is buried.

Other important metropolitan areas in Argentina include Córdoba (population 1,179,420) in the central section; Rosario (population 1,157,372), inland from Buenos Aires on the Paraná River; Mendoza (population 801,920), near the border with Chile; La Plata (population 676,128), southeast of Buenos Aires; and Tucumán (population 642,473) in the northwest.

Arts and Literature

Music, writing, drama, sculpture, and painting have blossomed in Argentina, especially in and around Buenos Aires, although repressive regimes have often attempted to deter their free expression. Music is a very important part of Argentine life . Perhaps the most famous musical form in Argentina is the all-important *tango,* a stylized dance and type of music that originated in Buenos Aires. The tango is a ballroom dance that developed from the *milonga,* a "disreputable" dance of the lower and working classes in the capital city. The upper classes viewed the milonga with scorn because of its suggestiveness and sensuality. The tango, polished and refined for the popular taste, became socially acceptable at the turn of the century and was all the rage in Europe before 1920. Such entertainers as Carlos Gardel acquired great international fame singing the songs that accompany tango music.

Opera is also a passion of many porteños, who attend the grand Teatro Colón, the most important of the city's theaters. Opened in 1908, the opera house has been the site of performances by world-renowned singers, from Enrico Caruso in the 1910s to Placido Domingo in the 1990s. The opera season runs for eight months, and the rest of the year the theater houses both the National Sym-

Patti LuPone portrayed Evita Perón in the 1979 musical Evita! *The musical was extremely successful, to the dismay of some Argentines who felt it romanticized and simplified the first Peronist period.*

phony Orchestra and the National Ballet, two outstanding companies. Another focus of musical life in Argentina is the Buenos Aires Conservatory, which was founded in 1893 by Alberto Williams, one of Argentina's most famous composers. Many concert pieces based on Argentine themes have been performed at the conservatory.

Since the return of democracy to Argentina, numerous expatriate singers have returned to their native country. Mercedes Sosa, who has performed throughout Europe and has also played to cheering audiences at New York's Carnegie Hall, was warmly received at the Teatro Colón upon her return to Argentina. Horacio Guarani also returned to Buenos Aires amid great excitement, bringing his deeply political songs expressing strong disagreement with military government.

Buenos Aires is home not only to such vital cultural institutions as the Teatro Colón but also to many museums that reveal the history and culture of Argentina. The National Museum of Fine Arts has a large collection of both Argentine and foreign works. Among the capital's other museums are the Municipal Museum and the Isaac Fernando Blanco Museum of Spanish-American Art. The excellent Museum of Modern Art is located in the city of Rosario.

In recent years Argentina and Argentine culture have become more popular throughout the world. In the late 1970s the musical *Evita!*, by British composer Andrew Lloyd Webber, was a big hit, capturing numerous awards and winning the hearts of theater audiences, first on Broadway in New York City, then throughout the United States. The musical romanticized the life of Eva Perón, and it upset many Argentines, who felt it glorified and simplified a part of their history that was much less glamorous and far more complicated than it appeared on the stage. Despite these complaints, the musical was turned into a movie in 1996, starring the American pop singer Madonna as Eva Perón.

Literature has also flourished in Argentina. Its writers include Jorge Luis Borges (1899–1986), who achieved great international acclaim. His works have been compared to those of Edgar Allan Poe and Franz Kafka. Two of his most important short-story collections are *Ficciones* (Fictions) and *El Aleph* (the aleph is the first letter in the Hebrew alphabet), which both portray, in fantastic stories, the world as a large labyrinth. The atmosphere of many of Borges's tales can be compared to that of the "Twilight Zone" television series. Many of his works are available in English.

Domingo Faustino Sarmiento, one of Argentina's greatest 19th-century writers and president from 1868 to 1871, was the author of the highly popular *Facundo*. This book called for a restructuring of pampean life that would leave little room for the gaucho and his rugged existence. Interestingly enough, as the gaucho himself faded away and became more a part of history, his legend grew dramatically. Sarmiento's book was a mixture of fact and fiction, romance and history, and had a great effect on later generations.

In addition to Borges, Argentina has produced a number of other important 20th-century writers. Adolfo Bioy Caseres chronicled the porteño experience in works such as *Asleep in the Sun*. Julio Cortázar (1916–84) was a writer who settled in Paris after he left his Argentine homeland when Perón began to limit artistic expression there. He was the author of one of the most important Latin American novels of the century, *Rayuela* (Hopscotch, 1963), as well as a master of the short story. One of his stories became the basis for the prize-winning film *Blow Up* (1966). Manuel Puig is the author of the novel *Kiss of the Spider Woman*, which was made into a film that won the Academy Award for Best Picture in 1986.

Argentina also left its mark on the North American film world when Argentine Norma Aleandro garnered a Best Actress nomination for her work in *The Official Story*. She portrayed a woman living in Buenos Aires who becomes aware of the plight of los Desaparecidos and decides to rebel against authority. *The Mission*

Jorge Luis Borges visited Edgar Allan Poe's grave in Baltimore in 1983. Borges, who was blind, was photographed running his hand over a plaque commemorating Poe. Some readers and critics see similarities between the two writers; it certainly seems that Borges admired Poe's work.

was an acclaimed film that detailed the story of the Jesuit missionaries' attempts to convert the Indians and featured beautiful photography of the Iguazú Falls. Argentina's native film industry continues to grow, spurred on by the help of such prominent producers as Leopoldo Torre-Nilsson, but American and European films are still the people's favorites.

Sports and Recreation

Argentines may love to read, dance, and see movies, but their true recreational love is soccer, the great sport of the people. Soccer is as common in Argentina as baseball is in America, and Argentine children grow up on soccer the way American children grow up on

Little League baseball. One of Argentina's greatest moments in soccer came when the national team won the World Cup in 1986, a victory that will be celebrated for many years to come. Led by the international star Diego Maradona, they defeated West Germany as the entire world watched.

Soccer superstar Diego Armando Maradona evades an opponent on the way to his second goal in the semifinal World Cup match in Mexico City in 1986. Argentina defeated Belgium in the semifinal and West Germany in the final to gain the coveted trophy.

Throughout Argentina's history the horse has played a central role in its culture. From the gaucho to the modern estancia owner, equestrian ability is greatly esteemed by the Argentines. Although at least in urban areas cars and trucks have replaced the horse as a means of transport, this animal still holds a high place in the recreation of the modern Argentine.

Horse racing is pursued with a passion throughout the country, but nowhere is it as glamorous and international as at Palermo. Palermo is a beautiful track that draws up to 40,000 people each day. Argentine polo players and their finely bred horses compete in leagues throughout the world, wherever polo is played. These international stars begin their training as children in leagues similar to those for soccer.

Pato ("duck" in Spanish) is another sport played on horseback, using a ball in a six-handled leather harness. The goal is to hurl the ball, or pato, at a net. The name *pato* originates from the earliest games when a real duck was used instead of a ball and was thrown through an iron hoop three feet (one meter) in diameter. The riders use special saddles that enable them to maneuver on the horse so that they can pick up the pato while riding at high speeds. Horses similar to polo ponies are used because of their speed, endurance, and agility.

Other major sports include tennis (Argentina has produced such stars as Guillermo Vilas and Gabriela Sabatini), basketball, and rugby, a British-influenced sport similar to football that is growing increasingly popular.

Another central part of Argentina's cultural life is *fiestas* (festivals), regional celebrations that are steeped in music, dance, food, and tradition. In the north, carnival, a huge party on Fat Tuesday, the day before Lent (the period of fasting before Easter), is widely celebrated with exuberant dancing, drinking, and huge parades, not unlike Mardi Gras in New Orleans.

Most of Argentina's traditional dishes revolve around beef. *Asado*, or barbecue, is the most popular and an asado for many people often turns into a party. Other favorites include *churrasco* (grilled steak), *ossobuco* (beef stew), *puchero de gallina* (chicken stew), *empanadas* (stuffed pastries), and *a caballo*, a steak topped with a fried egg.

In Mendoza, a wine-growing region along the Andes, the Vendimia Festival in May is very important, celebrating the wine harvest and honoring the more than 1,500 wine producers in the region. During the winter (June through September in the Southern Hemisphere) the mountains of this region provide the Argentine people with many opportunities to enjoy one of their favorite cold-weather sports, skiing.

Architecture

Excellent examples of colonial architecture have been preserved throughout the northern part of Argentina. The cathedral in Córdoba, begun in the 16th century and finished in 1784, is perhaps the finest example of religious colonial architecture in Argentina. The northeastern province of Misiones boasts many ruins from Jesuit missions in the area. Many of the altars and ornaments in the churches of Buenos Aires come from this region.

Much of the architecture in the center of Buenos Aires was built in the 19th century, including the Casa Rosada and the Palace of Congress. The rash of building in Buenos Aires accompanied the vigorous growth of Argentine society in that century. Like the people, much of this architecture had its roots in Europe. Both Spanish and Italian architecture affected Argentine design, which often incorporates in urban spaces gardens featuring marble statues and busts.

One of Argentina's more modern structures is the General San Martín Cultural Center in Buenos Aires. Its fine woodwork and modern lighting help to illuminate one of the centers of the city. Its many areas and salons include lecture halls, art exhibition spaces, and complex audiovisual and photographic rooms, and the center is home to the LS1 Municipal Radio Station, the Municipal Tourism Board, the Municipal Cinema Museum, and the Music Conservatoire Manuel de Falla, named after the Spanish composer who lived in Córdoba during the last years of his life.

A Buenos Aires billboard envisions a bright future for the city's port. Yet, to take advantage of the country's strengths, the Argentine government will need to solve chronic economic problems.

8

Argentina's Future

Argentina is filled with hope for the future. Its vast area and abundant natural resources should equip its well-educated population to face the 21st century with a great deal of optimism. Democracy has fueled that optimism since 1983, but a chronically restless military and economic uncertainty still threaten the nation's potential. The country has taken steps to expand democratic freedoms and reduce the size and power of the military. But if the economy continues to suffer, some sectors of Argentine society may once again start placing their hopes in dictatorial solutions.

In foreign affairs, Argentina has attempted in recent years to develop new ties and repair some strained relationships. In 1990 full diplomatic relations with Great Britain were restored for the first time since 1982. Since that time, the two countries have signed several agreements aimed at cooperating on the future of the Falkland Islands despite their continued disagreements. (Argentina continues to claim sovereignty over the islands.) Following the discovery of potentially rich petroleum deposits in the region, Argentina and Great Britain agreed in 1995 to cooperate in exploring for oil. Negotiations have also begun between the two countries to reach an agreement regarding fishing rights.

In 1991 the presidents of Argentina, Brazil, Paraguay, and Uruguay signed a treaty that led to the creation of the Southern Cone Common Market (MERCOSUR) in 1995. In agreeing to drop trade barriers between their countries, they hoped to increase regional commerce, to the benefit of each member country.

But as commerce expands, Argentina must face the ecological threats that increased technological development brings. Encouraging the rapid use of resources almost always generates negative side effects along with temporary economic gain. In order to increase their yields, farmers continue to use large amounts of pest-killing chemicals, some of which hurt the environment. If they continue to dust crops (to spray weed killers and insecticides over large areas with airplanes) and hunt and trap the diverse animal life of the pampa beyond reasonable limits, some species of Argentina's wildlife population may soon dwindle to extinction.

Pollution problems accompany the use of other natural resources as well. On January 28, 1989, a major oil spill occurred when the Argentine polar supply ship *Bahia Taraiso* ran aground off the Antarctic peninsula. The leaking oil washed ashore on many nearby islands, killing many krill (shrimplike animals that are food for fish, birds, and whales). The spill endangered the life of more than 30,000 seabirds, including gulls, penguins, and cormorants. The spill remained a problem for almost two months, until the Argentine navy finished the cleanup on March 23. This spill dramatically pointed out the need for responsible control over resource exploitation and for effective emergency response teams.

Argentina is trying to open up its southern sector to expanded economic use. Following the example of its neighbor Brazil, which attempted to shift its population inland from the coast by building the new capital of Brasília in the interior, Argentines have discussed moving Argentina's capital from Buenos Aires to Viedma in the south in an effort to open up that region to economic development. Urban overcrowding in Buenos Aires and the desire to spread wealth and power throughout the nation instead of having it concentrated in Buenos Aires are also motivations for this important plan.

The wisdom of such a move is questionable. The Brazilian experiment has failed. Since the capital was moved there in 1960, the population has shifted—but not to the area surrounding Brasília. Instead, Brazil's industrial center remains the old capital of Rio de Janeiro and

Nahuel Huapi National Park, near the ski resort of Bariloche, is part of the effort to preserve Argentina's natural beauty in the face of increasing exploitation of its wealth of resources.

Not only the artists' district of Buenos Aires, shown here, but many other aspects of Argentine culture have flourished in recent years.

its neighboring city to the south, São Paolo, and the migrants to the new capital area have succeeded only in altering the fragile ecology of the Amazon River basin. There is no guarantee that Viedma would have a similar fate, but Brazil's experience is not encouraging. Because of such doubts, no plans have been made to move the Argentine capital anytime soon.

Following his election in 1989, President Carlos Saúl Menem introduced a series of tough economic measures that were intended to control inflation, cut government spending, and restructure payments on Argentina's enormous foreign debt. Within a couple of years, progress was being made on all of these goals. The government sold several state-owned companies to private investors, including the national airline and the state oil company. By 1993 the inflation rate had dropped below 10 percent, and foreign investment in the country was rising.

When Menem was re-elected in 1995, he claimed that his principal goals would be creating new jobs and expanding social justice. A continuing consequence of his drastic economic policies, however, has been the growing income gap between rich and poor. Opposition to economic austerity has provoked reaction, some of it violent. In June 1996, the opposition Radical Civic Union won the first-ever election for mayor of Buenos Aires. This was seen as a sign of voter dissatisfaction with Menem and his Justicialist party.

Compared with other South American nations, Argentina's industrial work force is large and its poverty level low. The country has advantages in natural resources, education, and modernization over many of its neighbors. Its culture has flourished in recent years, and Argentine dance, cinema, arts, and literature are popular around the globe. The opportunity therefore exists for Argentina to become a major force in the world, but the country has yet to find a secure position within the world economy that would allow it to prosper. The success of its still relatively young commitment to democracy may well depend on its finding a way for all Argentines to benefit.

GLOSSARY

altiplano	A high plateau, found in the Puna region.
bola	A weapon made of rope with three balls at the end, used to catch animals.
cabildo	Town council or local government; also, the central authority of a Spanish colonial city.
Casa Rosada	Pink House, the president's palace in Buenos Aires.
creole	A person of European descent born in the colonies.
los Descamisados	The Shirtless Ones, in Spanish; followers of Perón, often members of the working class.
los Desaparecidos	The Disappeared Ones; people arrested by members of the military security forces in the 1970s and 1980s. Many of these people were arrested secretly, then tortured and murdered.
estancias	Large ranches on the pampa; their owners are called *estancieros*.
fiestas	Regional celebrations or festivals.
Guerra Sucia	Dirty War; a conflict in the late 1970s between left-wing guerrillas and the military.

el Líder   The Leader, a popular nickname for Perón in the 1940s.

inflation   An economic term that refers to rising prices resulting from an excess amount of money in circulation.

mestizo   A person of mixed European and Indian ancestry.

Nunca Más   A report issued in September of 1974 concerning the human rights violations of the military government in the 1970s.

pato   A popular sport in Argentina in which a ball in a six-handled leather harness is thrown at a net. The game is played on horseback.

porteños   People of Buenos Aires and the surrounding metropolitan area.

La Prensa   The leading independent newspaper in Argentina.

quebracho   A tree that is very common in the Chaco province. It is used to make tannin.

vaqueros   Groups of men who went out to hunt wild cattle during the 16th century.

yerba mate   A tealike liquid drunk from a gourd, sipped through a *bombilla*, or metal straw. The drink was especially popular with gauchos.

INDEX

121

126

Springsteen, Bruce, 20
Staten Island, 25
Sting, 20
Stroessner, Alfredo, 61

T
Talas tree, 27
Tango, 103–4, 105
Tannin, 26
Tapirs, 28, 29
Teatro Colón, 104, 105
Tennis, 19, 109
Thatcher, Margaret, 66
Tierra del Fuego, 23, 30, 38
Tierra del Fuego Archipelago,
 25
Tlatelolco, Treaty of, 83
Toledo, Francisco de, 40
Torre-Nilsson, Leopoldo, 107
Tucumán, 103
Tucumán, University of, 87

U
Unitarists, 46
United Nations, 84
United States, 32, 47, 57, 72, 83, 87,
 92, 93, 101, 107
*Universal Declaration of Human
 Rights, The*, 20
Uriburu, José F., 53
Uruguay, 38, 43, 48, 64, 83

Uruguay River, 26, 38, 92, 95
U.S. Bill of Rights, 72
U.S. Constitution, 71, 72, 81
Ushuaia, 30

V
Valdés Peninsula, 32
Vaqueros, 40
Vatican, 30
Vendimia Festival, 110
Venezuela, 45
Viceroyalty of La Plata, 43, 46
Vicuña, 25–26, 29
Videla, Jorge, 68
Viedma, 18, 114, 116
Vilas, Guillermo, 109
Viola, Roberto, 63, 68
Vizcacha, 29, 33

W
Washington, George, 45
Webber, Andrew Lloyd, 105
West Germany, 108
Williams, Alberto, 105
World Cup (1986), 108
World War II, 53, 54, 57

Y
Yagane Indians, 30
Yahgan Indians, 38
Yerba mate, 43, 100